Utilizing E
Spiritual Roots
for
Recovery Today

Dick B.

Paradise Research Publications, Inc.
Kihei, Maui, Hawaii

Paradise Research Publications, Inc., P.O. Box 837, Kihei, HI
96753-0837

This Paradise Research Publications, Inc., Edition is published
by arrangement with Good Book Publishing Company, P.O.
Box 837, Kihei, HI 96753-0837

Cover Design: Lili Crawford (Maui Cyber Design)

The publication of this volume does not imply affiliation with
nor approval or endorsement from Alcoholics Anonymous
World Services, Inc.

Publisher's Cataloging in Publication

B., Dick.
    Utilizing Early A.A.'s Spiritual Roots for Recovery Today /
  Dick. B.--Second impression.
    p. cm.
    ISBN: 1-885803-28-1
    1. Alcoholics Anonymous--History. 2. Alcoholism--Treatment--
    United States. I. Title
Preassigned Library of Congress Catalog Card No.: 99-93032

Utilizing Early A.A.'s Spiritual Roots for Recovery Today

Dick B
2005

Other Titles by Dick B.

Dr. Bob and His Library

Anne Smith's Journal, 1933-1939:
A.A.'s Principles of Success

The Oxford Group & Alcoholics Anonymous:
A Design for Living That Works

The Akron Genesis of Alcoholics Anonymous

New Light on Alcoholism:
God, Sam Shoemaker, and A.A.

The Books Early AAs Read for Spiritual Growth

Courage to Change (with Bill Pittman)

The Good Book and The Big Book:
A.A.'s Roots in the Bible

That Amazing Grace:
The Role of Clarence and Grace S. in Alcoholics Anonymous

Good Morning!:
Quiet Time, Morning Watch, Meditation, and Early A.A.

Turning Point:
A History of A.A.'s Spiritual Roots and Successes

HOPE!: The Story of Geraldine D., Alina Lodge & Recovery

The Golden Text of A.A.:
God, the Pioneers, and Real Spirituality

By the Power of God:
A Guide to Early A.A. Groups & Forming Similar Groups Today

Contents

1

The Spiritual Beginnings of A.A.

A.A. is a spiritual program. What that means is questionable. Some AAs say their entire program is spiritual. Most would agree A.A. offers a spiritual solution to alcoholism.

Dr. Bob and His Bible

We believe A.A. spirituality began in the youth of its co-founder Dr. Bob (Dr. Robert Holbrook Smith). From childhood through high school, Bob went to church, Sunday school and evening service, Monday-night Christian Endeavor, and sometimes to Wednesday evening prayer meeting. Years later, in his last major A.A. address (*The Co-founders of Alcoholics Anonymous: Biographical Sketches Their Last Major Talks*), Bob recalled of A.A.'s beginnings:

> I had refreshed my memory of the Good Book [the Bible], and I had had excellent training in that as a youngster (pp. 11-12).

> I'm somewhat allergic to work, but I felt that I should increase my familiarity with the Good Book and also should read a good deal of standard literature, possibly of a scientific nature (p. 13).

> . . . [W]e were convinced that the answer to our problems was in the Good Book (p. 13).

> We got them [the Twelve Steps], as I said, as a result of our study of the Good Book (p. 14)

A.A.'s biography of Dr. Bob (*DR. BOB and the Good Oldtimers*) says:

> If someone asked him a question about the program, his usual response was: "What does it say in the Good Book?" (p. 144).

> He cited the Sermon on the Mount as containing the underlying spiritual philosophy of A.A. (p. 228).

A.A.'s other founder Bill Wilson agreed as to Jesus's sermon. Of Dr. Bob, Bill said:

> And I sort of depended on him to get me into heaven. Bob was far ahead of me in that sort of activity. I was always rushing around talking and organizing and "teaching kindergarten." I never grew up myself.

Bill said he and Bob never quarreled, and that was true concerning A.A.'s roots in the Bible. Bill once told T. Henry Williams (an early Oxford Group activist) that he had known very little about the Bible until he came to Akron and studied it with Dr. Bob, Bob's wife Anne, Henrietta Seiberling, and T. Henry Williams and T. Henry's wife Clarace.

A.A.'s Akron Genesis in 1931

Akron, Ohio's tire magnate Harvey Firestone, Sr., had a son named Russell who had a severe alcoholism problem. In 1928, Harvey, Sr., brought to Akron a young protege named James D. Newton, grooming Newton for Firestone Tire and Rubber Company leadership. Newton befriended Russell, became aware of Russell's drinking problem, and sought to help.

Consequently, in 1931, Newton and at least three members of the Firestone family (Harvey, Sr., Leonard, and Russell) met with Newton's friend, Reverend Samuel M. Shoemaker, Jr., rector of Calvary Episcopal Church in New York City. Russell was persuaded to join the group on a trip to an Episcopal Bishop's Conference in Denver. On the train, Russell drank at least a quart a day. Newton had previously spent considerable time with Russell, coaching him in the life changing program of A First Century Christian Fellowship also known as the Oxford Group. Shoemaker, a crack life-changer and major spokesman for the Oxford Group in America, led Russell to a decision for Christ during the return trip. The result was electric and miraculous. Firestone's own physician saw an immediate recovery in Russell.

Russell and Jim Newton thereafter witnessed at many Oxford Group meetings for several years. In 1933, Newton, the Firestones, and Dr. Walter Tunks, rector of the St. Paul's Church in Akron, invited Oxford Group Founder Dr. Frank N. D. Buchman to bring a "team" of Oxford Group adherents to Akron to witness about God's delivering power. For ten days, the group spoke at public meetings and church pulpits and told their personal stories about what God had done for them when they surrendered their lives to His care and direction. The newspapers in Akron widely publicized the events.

Four ladies (Dr. Bob's wife Anne, Henrietta Seiberling, Clarace Williams, and Delphine Weber) attended the events, which culminated in a huge meeting in Akron's Mayflower Hotel. The elite of Akron, as well as a good many clergymen, were present. And the four ladies not only aligned themselves with the Oxford Group, but persuaded Dr. Bob to join with them. As Bob put it, from January of 1933 till the time he met Wilson in the spring of 1935, Bob read an immense amount of Oxford Group literature, attended meetings, went to church, prayed, studied the Bible, *and drank*!

Then a change occurred in the spring of 1935. At the instance of Henrietta Seiberling (wife of rubber magnate Frank Seiberling's son John), a special Oxford Group meeting was called at T. Henry Williams's home. Its avowed purpose was to help Bob overcome his drinking problem. All present confessed their shortcomings. Dr. Bob followed suit by sharing his drinking problem. He was asked if he wished to pray. He dropped to his knees, and all present prayed for his deliverance. He continued to drink. *For a short time!*

Then, in an unpredictable visit to Akron which most believe to be the answer to prayer, an Oxford Group drunk from New York arrived and sought out a drunk to help. The "rum hound from New York," as he called himself, was Bill Wilson. The person who brought Bill and Dr. Bob together was Henrietta Seiberling; and Henrietta called Bill's appearance "manna from heaven." The two drunks got together, hit it off well, and began a four year spiritual experiment which produced a basic textbook, Twelve Steps, and the A.A. Fellowship.

A.A.'s Switzerland roots in 1931

Akron A.A.'s spiritual beginnings started circuitously via Jim Newton, the Firestones, and Sam Shoemaker. Similarly, New York A.A.'s beginnings started circuitously in 1931. Rowland Hazard, a Rhode Island scion, was an alcoholic. He sought help in Switzerland in 1931 from the famous psychiatrist Dr. Carl G. Jung in Switzerland. The treatments failed. But Jung advised Rowland that he needed a religious conversion experience. Jung called it "union with God." Jung suggested Rowland join a religious group. And Rowland aligned himself with the Oxford Group. He had a conversion experience, learned the Oxford Group's biblical principles, passed them on to an Albany alcoholic named Ebby Thacher, aligned himself with Rev. Sam Shoemaker's Calvary Episcopal Church in New York, and actually counseled Bill Wilson for several years.

Ebby Thacher had known Bill Wilson for years. Ebby had visited Calvary Church's Rescue Mission, made a decision for Christ, and then witnessed to his old drinking friend Bill. Wilson also sought out Calvary Rescue Mission, there made a decision for

Christ, and several times wrote that he had been born again "for sure." In just a few days, Bill got sober at Towns Hospital where he had often been treated for alcoholism. Bill dived into Oxford Group activity, began feverishly working with alcoholics, but was completely unsuccessful (in his six months of "oxfordizing" in New York) in leading *anyone* to sobriety.

However, Bill did establish strong Christian connections with several Oxford Group mentors such as Rowland Hazard, Shep Cornell, Ebby, the Rev. Sam Shoemaker, Shoemaker's circle of clergy and the lay people in Shoemaker's church who helped Bill help drunks.

Bill was later to confess that his New York drunks never quite emphasized the "spiritual" enough. In the four or five years he had drunks in his home, not one got sober. But, with six months of sobriety under his belt, Bill did go to Akron, thinking there of drinking. His six months of witnessing, however, stopped him dead in his tracks. Bill looked up Dr. Walter Tunks, Rector of St. Paul's Church in Akron and was put in touch with Henrietta Seiberling who put Bill in touch with Dr. Bob in a meeting at her home which catalyzed A.A.'s ideas.

The Akron Experiment and A.A.'s Spiritual Program

Akron's founding in Dr. Bob's Akron home about June 10, 1935 (when Dr. Bob took his last drink) is well-reported history. The spiritual picture is not.

Bill moved into the Smith home at 855 Ardmore Avenue and stayed there for three months in the summer of 1935. Bill and Bob began regularly attending Oxford Group meetings together with Anne Smith and Henrietta Seiberling. Meetings were held at the home of Oxford Group activists T. Henry and Clarace Williams. The Bible was studied. Quiet Time was observed. Meetings began and ended with prayer. Christian literature was distributed and read. Surrender to Jesus Christ as Lord and Savior was a must.

The Oxford Group's life-changing principles became the structure for Bill Wilson's famous Twelve Steps (which he wrote in 1938 as he assembled A.A.'s textbook). The Oxford Group maintained that its principles were the principles of the Bible. And so they were, albeit Protestant in orientation. Shoemaker's Christian books on surrender, life-changing, quiet time, the new birth, prayer, the Bible, how to find God, restitution, conversion, witnessing, and fellowship were almost completely swallowed by the fledgling alcoholic program, not only in Akron, but in New York.

Dr. Bob's wife Anne jotted down all the materials that the Oxford Group people, the pioneer alcoholics, and their families were learning about the Oxford Group principles, the Bible, the available literature, and practical living. Anne assembled her spiritual journal over the years from 1933 to 1939. She shared its contents with early AAs, their wives, and their families. Anne had *been* a teacher, and she *was* a teacher, from the Bible, the literature, and her journal. In sixty-four pages, Anne set down the Biblical ideas and Oxford Group principles and practices that became the heart of A.A. spiritual ideas. Not surprisingly, Bill Wilson called Anne Smith the "Mother of A.A." and a "founder."

The materials in the devotionals the pioneers used reinforced the biblical and fellowship aspects of the early program. The Bible was the core. The Oxford Group program was the structure for life-change and conversion. The Bible devotionals and prayers were the heart of daily life. Anne Smith's journal was a reference tool that faithfully recorded it all.

A.A.: Spiritual or Religious?

AAs often say today that their program "is spiritual, not religious." Yet, as A.A. oldtimer and historian Mel B. observes: "If pressed for what the program's actual definition of *spiritual* is, however, it's doubtful that many AA members could explain." *Merriam Webster's Collegiate Edition* defines *religion* as "the service and worship of God or the supernatural." A.A.'s basic text speaks with great reverence of "God," service to God, and conforming to His will. A.A.'s text (*Alcoholics Anonymous*) refers to God in one way or another, with capital letters, over 400 times. *Webster's* defines *Christianity* as "the religion derived from Jesus Christ, based on the Bible as sacred scripture, and professed by Eastern, Roman Catholic, and protestant bodies."

As seen, Dr. Bob was much involved in Christian bodies in his youth. About 1933, he became an adherent of "A First Century Christian Fellowship," also known as the Oxford Group. With his wife Anne, at about the same time, he became a charter member of a Presbyterian Church in Akron and remained a member through A.A.'s developmental years. Shortly before his death, he became a communicant of St. Paul's Protestant Episcopal Church in Akron. He studied the Bible intensely for two and a half years before he met Bill. When the two teamed up, they were an integral part of the Christian Oxford Group. They studied the Bible together. They had quiet time and prayer together. They read Christian literature together. By any definition, in the early days, therefore, A.A. was *religious*! Perhaps even a religion. And the famous preacher and friend of A.A. Harry Emerson Fosdick so observed.

The story as to Bill himself is somewhat different. His secretary Nell Wing was and is fond of saying that Bill was not a religious person, but spiritual. In his youth, Bill turned from religion. But AAs seem to have forgotten many facts about his early A.A. days. He made a decision for Christ at Shoemaker's Rescue Mission. He said he had been born again. He was much involved in the Oxford Group. He told a Yale audience that most AAs (including himself) were practicing Christians. He said the Rev. Sam Shoemaker had taught him most of the Christian principles that AAs borrowed for their program. He attributed most of A.A.'s ideas to the inspiration of the clergy. He studied Christian Science. He counseled with Shoemaker. Then he aligned himself with the Roman Catholic Jesuit Priest Father Ed Dowling as his "sponsor." He had the Roman Catholic theologian Father John Ford, S.J., thoroughly edit A.A.'s *Twelve Steps and Twelve Traditions* and *Alcoholics Anonymous Comes of Age*. And he took Roman Catholic instruction from Monsignor Fulton J. Sheen and seriously considered converting to Roman Catholicism. How religious can one get! But certain events were to change the A.A. fellowship itself.

Early on, Roman Catholic clergy had distaste for the Oxford Group. Bill developed Twelve Traditions offering A.A. as a haven for all religious persuasions, *even none*. Dr. Bob was not supportive, but died agreeing. Bill spoke more of a "higher power." A.A.'s Fellowship became *less* religious, presumably "spiritual," and now openly welcomes *any* suffering drunk.

2

The Bible in Early A.A.

Early A.A. had six verifiable and often mentioned spiritual sources. As Dr. Bob pointed out, the basic ideas came from the Bible. The Bible was the core, and the other five sources supplemented that biblical, "spiritual side." The other roots were: (1) Quiet Time, Morning Watch, and meditation; (2) The Oxford Group program; (3) The Reverend Samuel Shoemaker's influence; (4) The role of Anne Smith ("Mother of A.A."); and (5) Christian literature of the 1930's.

Biblical "Essentials" A.A.'s Pioneers Emphasized

The Sermon on the Mount

According to founders Bill and Dr. Bob, the Sermon on the Mount (Matthew, Chapters 5, 6, and 7) contained the underlying philosophy of A.A. As you review the Twelve Steps, you can see the verses that found their way directly into the recovery ideas. But there was probably one core idea that started the ball rolling. Likening the man who heard his sayings and did them, to one who built his house upon a rock, Jesus taught in Matthew 7:21:

Not everyone that saith unto me, Lord, Lord, shall enter into the kingdom of heaven; but he that doeth the will of my Father which is in heaven.

Emphasizing this importance of doing the will of God, AAs adopted the Lord's Prayer (Matthew 6:10-13) from Jesus's sermon and frequently quoted (in their basic text) the part which reads: "Thy will be done . . ." (Matthew 6:10). Jesus was explaining to his disciples on the mount a number of God's commandments, to which A.A. pioneers subscribed: (1) Avoiding anger (Matthew 5:22); (2) Making amends (Matthew 5:23-24); (3) Promptly admitting wrong (Matthew 5:25-26); (4) Eschewing adultery (Matthew 5:27-32); and (5) "Turning the other cheek" by making peace, avoiding resentment, and resisting retaliation (Matthew 5:29-48).

There were still more ideas taken from the sermon: (1) Avoiding hypocritical and ostentatious worship, prayers, and gifts; and rendering service to God and others "anonymously" (Matthew 6:1-24); (2) Seeking and relying on God's help *first* (Matthew 6:25-33); (3) Focusing on the problems of each day without anxiety (Matthew 6:34); (4) Looking for one's own part in wrongdoing (Matthew 7:1-5); (5) Looking to God as One who gives good things and answers prayers (Matthew 7:7-11); (6) Doing unto others as you would have them do to you—the "golden rule" (Matthew 7:12). Such conduct, said Jesus, constituted building one's house on the reliable rock of conformity to God's will.

1 Corinthians 13—"the greatest of these is love"

When one looks for the "principles" which AAs were to practice, there is little doubt that Dr. Bob regarded "love and service" as the essence of the Twelve Steps. He placed great store in the words of the so-called "love" chapter found in 1 Corinthians 13.

There is much there, and many of the old English words are difficult to understand. However, Dr. Bob highly recommended

Professor Henry Drummond's little pamphlet called *The Greatest Thing in the World*. There Drummond lays out what he calls the nine ingredients of love as they are set forth in 1 Corinthians 13:4-6.

These ingredients can be found in A.A.'s basic text. They are (1) Patience; (2) Kindness; (3) Generosity (or, as rendered in A.A., absence of envy); 4) Humility; (5) Courtesy; (6) Unselfishness; (7) Good temper; (8) Guilelessness (perhaps better thought of as not adding up grievances and retaliating); and (9) Sincerity (perhaps better thought of in terms of the "rigorous honesty" to which A.A. subscribes).

Patience, tolerance, kindness, and love are A.A. watchwords. Humility is often the topic at A.A. meetings. Honesty is given great attention in A.A.'s Big Book. Unselfishness is also stressed. And making peace is an important aspect of A.A.'s recovery program.

The Book of James

Early AAs used Emmet Fox's *The Sermon on the Mount*, Oswald Chambers's *Studies in the Sermon on the Mount*, E. Stanley Jones's *The Christ of the Mount*, and Glenn Clark's books to help them study and interpret Matthew Chapters Five to Seven. They used Drummond's little pamphlet for assistance on 1 Corinthians 13. But no book was directly mentioned in connection with the Book of James although that book was often called the pioneers' favorite book in the Bible. However, *The Runner's Bible*, *The Upper Room*, and *My Utmost for His Highest* all contained frequent references to verses from James; and these devotionals were much used by A.A. pioneers.

There are some portions of James which have quite clear counterparts in A.A.'s Twelve Steps, Big Book, and Fellowship language.

See: (1) Patience (James 1:2-4; 5:7-8, 10-11); (2) Seeking God's guidance and wisdom with faith [believing] (James 1:4-8; 3:17-18); (3) Avoiding temptation (James 1:12-16); (4) the Father of lights [Bill used the expression Father of Light] (James 1:17); (5) Avoiding anger (James 1:19-20); (6) Bridling the tongue (James 1:26, 3:2-13); (7) Helping others (James 1:27-2:1-7; 3:1-17); (8) Faith without

works is dead (James, Chapter Two); (9) Avoiding envy and strife
(James 3:14-16); (10) Avoiding lying (James 3:14); (11) Making
peace (James 3:18); (11) Avoiding selfish prayer (James 4:1-7);
(12) Avoiding adultery (James 2:11, 3:4-6); (13) Submitting
yourself to God (James 4:7); (14) Drawing near to God so that He
will draw near to you (James 4:7); (15) Humbling yourself before
God (James 4:6, 10); (16) Avoiding evil gossip (James 4:11); (17)
Loving your neighbor as yourself (James 1:8); (18) Doing God's
will (James 4:14-15); (19) Avoiding grudges (James 5:9); (20)
Calling the elders to pray over, and obtain healing for, the sick
and for forgiveness of their sins (James 5:14-16); (21) Confessing
your faults to another (James 5:16); (22) Believing in the
effectiveness of prayer (James 5:16-18); (23) Converting sinners
from erroneous ways and saving their souls (James 5:19-20).

The Great Commandment

Frequently appearing in A.A. literature and talk are the concepts
of loving and serving God and loving and serving one's neighbor.
Matthew 22:36-40 states:

> Master, which *is* the great commandment in the law? Jesus said
> unto him, Thou shalt love the Lord thy God with all thy heart,
> and with all thy soul, and with all thy mind. This is the first and
> great commandment. And the second *is* like unto it, Thou shalt
> love thy neighbor as thyself. On these two commandments hang
> all the law and the prophets.

Other Biblical Roots

Early AAs drew every spiritual idea in the Twelve Steps—and
many in the Big Book—directly from the Bible. Some, unfortunately, were later scrapped. But AAs used biblical language to
refer to God as Creator, Maker, Spirit, Father, Father of lights,
God, God of our fathers, the living God, and God Almighty. They
stressed the necessity for belief in God (Hebrews 11:6). They
insisted on acceptance of Jesus Christ as Lord and Savior (Romans

10:9). They were a Christian fellowship (See Acts). They studied the Bible (2 Timothy 2:15). They used morning prayer and listened for guidance (Psalm 1:2; Psalm 5:1-3; Proverbs 3:5-6). They used Christian books to help them in prayer and spiritual growth (Compare Acts 8:26-40). They worked as a team and witnessed (Mark 16:4-20; Acts 4). They carried a message of salvation, forgiveness, power, healing, and deliverance (Acts 2:38-40; 3:17-16; 4:8-13, 30-31; 5:12; 8:5-13; 10:33-48). They looked to Psalms 23, 91, and 103 for affirmation that God is a loving, caring, protecting, guiding, forgiving, healing, delivering God.

In a moment, we will look at specific biblical ideas which AAs borrowed for their Twelve Steps. And here are some of the practical biblical principles by which they sought to live:

> Believing in God; Proving God's power by experimenting with their belief; Seeking God's will and guidance first; Examining their behavior for blocks to God; Confessing to another their errant behavior; Becoming convicted and repenting; Becoming converted through acceptance of Jesus as Lord; Concerning themselves with love and service to others; Setting things right with others; Continuing the process daily; Making Bible study, Quiet Time, prayer, guidance, and Christian fellowship a regular part of their day and lives; Renewing their minds to their new standing as God's children; Witnessing to, and helping others to, salvation and deliverance; Utilizing God's Word as their guide to doing God's will and living Christian precepts.

The fact is that the Christian literature the pioneers read, the devotionals they used each day, and the concepts they were hearing from the Oxford Group people and from Dr. Bob's wife Anne were consistently presenting well-known Bible segments and verses that gave rise to each of the principles embodied in the Twelve Steps. This is clear in part because the Oxford Group concepts, which were codified in the Twelve Steps, were drawn from specific portions of the Bible. And these same concepts were discussed in A.A.'s other root sources.

The Bible As the Main Source Book

A.A.'s biblical roots are not a matter of conjecture. They were specifically described by A.A.'s founders and teachers.

Dr. Bob said A.A.'s basic ideas came from study of the Bible. Bill Wilson reiterated the importance of the Sermon on the Mount, "Corinthians" (as he put it), and the book of James—saying "James was our favorite." He added: "The James Club" was favored by some as a name for the Fellowship. Dr. Bob's wife Anne, whom Wilson dubbed a "founder" of A.A., taught: "Of course the Bible ought to be the main Source Book of all. No day ought to pass without reading it." And none did in the early days at the Smith home, either when Bill was living there, or when AAs would gather at the Smith home in the mornings with Anne Smith for Quiet Time."

When John D. Rockefeller, Jr., dispatched A.A. trustee-to-be Frank Amos to Akron to investigate what was going on, Amos described the "Christian technique prescribed," saying of the alcoholic and the "Program":

> He must have devotions every morning—a "quiet time" of prayer and some reading from the Bible and other religious literature. Unless this is faithfully followed, there is grave danger of backsliding.

A.A.'s own historical materials make it clear that early meetings often opened with Bible reading conducted by Dr. Bob, Bill Dotson (A.A. Number Three), and others. The Bible was read during hospitalization, in the homes, at Quiet Times, and at meetings; and it was studied, discussed, and the subject of the religious literature being circulated. Oxford Group Founder Dr. Frank Buchman was said to be "soaked in the Bible" and insisted on Bible study by his adherents. Buchman's chief American lieutenant, The Reverend Sam Shoemaker, was called by his associates a "Bible Christian" and emphasized the Bible in his books, pamphlets, and articles which were read by the early AAs.

Specific Roots That Gave Rise to Specific Steps

Often, religious groups and others have pointed to specific Bible verses they believe "support" or seem "related" to particular steps. But the verses and segments that follow are mentioned in the Bible sources AAs themselves quoted or in the Christian literature they themselves read. The verses were mentioned in connection with the specific Twelve Step ideas set forth under each Step below. These, then, *are* specific sources of the particular Twelve Step ideas early AAs borrowed from the Bible.

Step One

"O wretched man that I am! who shall deliver me from the body of this death? I thank God through Jesus Christ our Lord . . . " (Romans 7:24-25).

Step Two

[Willingness] "If any man will do his will, he shall know of the doctrine, whether it be of God, or *whether* I speak of myself" (John 7:17).

> [Belief] But without faith, *it is* impossible to please *him*: for he that cometh to God

must believe that He is, and *that* he is a rewarder of them that diligently seek him" (Hebrews 11:6).

[Seeking] "But seek ye first the kingdom of God, and his righteousness; and all these things shall be added unto you" (Matthew 6:33).

Step Three

[Surrender] "That if thou shalt confess with thy mouth the Lord Jesus, and shalt believe in thine heart that God hath raised him from the dead, thou shalt be saved" (Romans 10:9). 'Give in,' he cries, 'admit that I am God, high over nations, high over the world'" (Moffatt's translation of Psalm 46:10); "Thy will be done" (Matthew 6:10).

Step Four

[Self-examination] "And why beholdest thou the mote [speck] that is in thy brother's eye, but considerest not the beam [log] that is in thine own eye? Or wilt thou say to thy brother, 'Let me pull out the mote out of thine eye;' and behold, a beam is in thine own eye? Thou hypocrite, first cast out the beam out of thine own eye; and then thou shalt see clearly to cast out the mote out of thy brother's eye" (Matthew 7:3-5).

Step Five

[Confidence and Confession] "Confess *your* faults one to another, and pray for one another, that ye may be healed" (James 5:16).

Step Six

[Conviction] "Against thee, thee only, have I sinned, and done *this* evil in thy sight . . . " (Psalm 51:4); "Iniquities prevail against me: as *for* our transgressions, thou shalt purge them away" (Psalm 65:3).

Step Seven

[Conversion] "Except a man be born again, he cannot see the kingdom of God" (John 3:3); "Submit yourselves therefore to God. Resist the devil, and he will flee from you" (James 4:7); "Humble yourselves in the sight of the Lord, and he shall lift you up" (James 4:10).

Step Eight

[Willingness as to amends] "Agree with thine adversary quickly, whiles thou art in the way with him . . . " (Matthew 5:25); "If a man say, I love God, and hateth his brother, he is a liar: for he that loveth not his brother whom he hath seen, how can he love God whom he hath not seen?" (1 John 4:20).

Step Nine

[Amends and Restitution] "Therefore if thou bring thy gift to the altar, and there rememberest that thy brother hath ought against thee; leave there thy gift before the altar, and go thy way; first be reconciled to thy brother, and then come and offer thy gift" (Matthew 5:23-24).

Step Ten

[Daily surrender] "Watch and pray, that ye enter not into temptation: the spirit indeed *is* willing, but the flesh *is* weak" (Matthew 26:4).

Step Eleven

[The effectiveness of prayer] "The effectual fervent prayer of a righteous man availeth much" (James 5:16).

[Evening review and correction] "And the prayer of faith shall save the sick, and the Lord shall raise him up; and if he have committed sins, they shall be forgiven him" (James 5:15); "If we confess our sins, he is faithful and just to forgive us *our* sins, and to cleanse us from all righteousness" (1 John 1:9).

[Morning guidance] "Speak, Lord; for thy servant heareth" (1 Samuel 3:9); "Lord, what wilt thou have me to do?" (Acts 9:6); "My voice shalt thou hear in the morning, O Lord; in the morning will I direct *my prayer* unto thee, and will look up" (Psalm 5:3); "Trust in the Lord with all thine heart; and lean not unto thine own understanding. In all thy ways acknowledge him, and he shall direct thy paths" (Proverbs 3:5-6).

[Spiritual growth] "Study to shew thyself approved unto God, a workman that needeth not to be ashamed, rightly dividing the word of truth" (2 Timothy 2:15).

[As to anxiety and doubt] "Thou wilt keep *him* in perfect peace, *whose* mind *is* stayed *on thee*: because he trusteth in thee" (Isaiah 26:3); "Thy will be done in earth, as it *is* in heaven" (Matthew 6:10); "Be careful [anxious] for nothing; but in everything by prayer and supplication with thanksgiving let your requests be made known unto God. And the peace of God, which passeth all understanding, shall keep your hearts and minds through Christ Jesus" (Philippians 4:6-7).

Step Twelve

[A spiritual experience] "But ye shall receive power, after that the Holy Ghost is come upon you: and ye shall be witnesses unto me both in Jerusalem, and in all Judaea, and in Samaria, and unto the uttermost part of the earth" (Acts 1:8); "Therefore if any man *be* in Christ, *he is* a new creature; old things are passed away; behold, all things are become new" (2 Corinthians 5:17).

[Passing it on] "But wilt thou know, O vain man, that faith without works is dead?" (James 2:20); "Come ye after me, and I will make you to become fishers of men" (Mark 1:17); "Now then we are ambassadors for Christ . . . " (2 Corinthians 5:20).

[Practicing Christian principles] "Though I speak with the tongues of men and of angels, and have not charity [love], I am become *as* sounding brass, or a tinkling cymbal. And though I have *the gift* of prophecy, and understand all mysteries, and all knowledge; and though I have all faith, so that I could remove mountains, and have not charity [love], I am nothing" (1 Corinthians 13:1-2). Early AAs adopted the "Four Absolutes" which were said to be a distillation of Jesus's teachings about moral standards. These pioneers endeavored to follow the precepts of the Sermon on the Mount, 1 Corinthians 13, and James. Also the Ten Commandments (Exodus 20:1-17).

What Is the Profit?

The importance of A.A.'s biblical roots has to do with understanding its program and the power which produced the early successes, the early design for living, and the zeal for passing it on. The drinking problem disappeared by the grace of God as early AAs tried to follow the will of God, be of maximum service to Him and others, and practice the love of God toward others. The latter is best expressed in 1 John 5:2-3:

> By this we know that we love the children of God, when we love God, and keep his commandments. For this is the love of God, that we keep his commandments: and his commandments are not grievous.

The Bible contains over 900 promises of God. It contains many commandments of love, culminating in Jesus's statement of the two great commandments: to love God and love our neighbor as ourselves—commandments that can be found in the Old Testament as well as the New Testament (See Deuteronomy 6:5; Leviticus 19:18).

The profit for AAs in knowing their biblical roots includes these points:

- God understands Himself and describes Himself meticulously in the Bible. If AAs want to understand the God upon which their founders relied, the Bible contains the facts.

- The only condition for coming to God and receiving His benefits is believing. If AAs want to seek the God who can and will deliver them, the Bible explains what to believe.

- The Bible shows the way to find or rediscover God through His son, Jesus Christ. If AAs want to follow the path of the pioneers, the Bible explains how.

- If AAs want to know the nature of the power that early AAs had, the Bible explains and illustrates the healing, forgiving, delivering, loving power of the Creator.

- If AAs want to know what the Big Book meant by such terms such as "Thy will be done," "Love thy neighbor as thyself," "faith without works is dead," "Creator," "Maker," "Father," "Spirit," and "fellowship," the Bible is the place to learn the details.

- When the Big Book speaks of seeking, learning, and obeying the will of God, the Bible not only sets forth God's will but shows how it can be learned from the Bible and by direct revelation. That is why early AAs looked to the Bible for guidance.

- When the Big Book speaks of "practicing the principles," those principles were set forth in the Four Absolutes (which came from the Bible), and in the other portions of the Bible we have mentioned.

- If one wishes to know how to pray as God would have him or her pray, the Bible contains specifics on the elements of prayer. It also shows which prayers are in accordance with Gods' will and which are not.

- Instead of speculating as to what is sin, "self-will," and God's will, AAs can look to the Bible which defined for the pioneers what was acceptable and what was not acceptable to God.

- If AAs wish to learn what the conversion experience was that formed the foundation for A.A. recovery, the Bible explains exactly what to do and what is received.

- If AAs wish to escape the guilt and shame and fear that abounds in the newcomer's thinking, the Bible offers promises and guarantees as to the grace and mercy of God.

One would hardly climb into a motor vehicle without instruction, without a license, and without an understanding of how to operate that vehicle. The same should be true for the grievously ill A.A. newcomer who needs to know how to find God *now*, as the Big Book suggests. Also how to ask for the things he or she needs and can expect to receive. The Bible contained the answers for early AAs, and the foregoing points suggest some major profit to all AAs today in knowing the biblical rock upon which their Twelve Steps stand.

3

Quiet Time, Morning Watch, and Meditation

An A.A. history quotes Bill Wilson as follows:

> I sort of always felt that something was lost from A.A. when we stopped emphasizing morning meditation (*DR. BOB and the Good Oldtimers*, p. 178).

Which raises the question: *What is it—this "morning meditation"*? Today's polyglot concoctions bear no resemblance to the "morning meditation" in A.A.'s early days. Early meditation ideas and practices came directly from the Bible. They involved *study* of the Word of God (the Bible). They involved *prayer to* God. They involved *listening for messages from God*. And They came to be called the "Morning Watch." Later, particularly in the Oxford Group, they came to be called "Quiet Time." And the "meditation" usually involved reading the Bible, praying to God, listening for messages from God, using Bible devotionals for assistance or inspiration when needed, writing down the thoughts which came, and checking those thoughts against the Bible, the teachings of Christ, and sometimes with other believers to avoid self-deception.

Early AAs consistently used "meditation" books which were called daily "devotionals," and each different devotional was quite similar to the next. These devotionals—usually pamphlets—set forth a verse for each day. Then a comment on the verse. Then other verses for further study. Then a thought for the day, and a prayer for the day. The whole Quiet Time observance usually took place in the early morning, but sometimes in meetings, in homes, and throughout the day where there was disquiet or anxiety.

Major Biblical Roots

As one looks at Quiet Time practices in early A.A., in the Oxford Group from which it sprang, and in the Christian literature early AAs read, it is very clear that each prayer and meditation idea had its roots in the Bible. And the following verses were commonly referred to in materials about Quiet Time.

Why Look to God's Word?

Psalm 119 was popular, and here are three verses that help to explain why meditation began with looking at the Good Book:

> Thy word *is* a lamp unto my feet, and a light unto my path (Psalm 119:105).

> The entrance of thy words giveth light; it giveth understanding unto the simple (Psalm 119:130).

> I will meditate in thy precepts, and have respect unto thy ways. I will delight myself in thy statutes: I will not forget thy word (Psalm 119:14-15).

Over and over, the Bible speaks of itself as the word of God, the word of the Lord, and the precepts or statutes or commandments or law of God. Collectively, the "words of God" were called the word of God. That word was spoken of as divinely inspired and profitable:

All scripture is given by inspiration of God, and *is* profitable for doctrine, for reproof, for correction, for instruction in righteousness (2 Timothy 3:16).

Morning Was the Time

Many verses emphasized the importance of rising with God:

Give ear to my words, O Lord, consider my meditation. Hearken unto the voice of my cry, my King, and My God: for unto thee will I pray. My voice shalt thou hear in the morning, O Lord; in the morning will I direct *my prayer* unto thee, and will look up (Psalm 5:3-5).

But I will sing of thy power; yea I will sing aloud of thy mercy in the morning: for thou hast been my defence and refuge in the day of my trouble (Psalm 59:16).

But unto thee have I cried, O Lord; and in the morning shall my prayer prevent [precede] thee (Psalm 88:13).

Other verses also emphasize this morning period of prayer, listening, and thanksgiving (Psalm 92:1-2; Psalm 143:8-11; Isaiah 50:4-5; Exodus 16:7).

Meditation Meant Focusing Thoughts, and Reflecting, on God's Word

Again the Psalms indicate that the focusing of thoughts, the reflection and pondering, the study had to do with the word of God, not some mindless chanting or sitting:

But his delight is in the law of the Lord; and in his law doth he meditate day and night (Psalm 1:2).

I will meditate in the precepts, and have respect unto thy ways. I will delight myself in thy statutes: I will not forget thy word (Psalm 119:15-16).

My hands also will lift up unto thy commandments, which I have loved; and I will meditate in thy statutes (Psalm 119:48).

Meditation Meant Study, Getting It Right, and Knowing!

The New Testament has these comments:

Search the scriptures; for in them ye think ye have eternal life: and they are they which testify of me (John 5:39).

Ye do err, not knowing the scriptures, nor the power of God (Matthew 22:19).

These [the believers from Berea] were more noble than those in Thessalonica, in that they received the word with all readiness of mind, and searched the scriptures daily, whether those things were so. Therefore many of them believed; also of honourable women which were Greeks, and of men, not a few (Acts 17:11-12).

Study to shew thyself approved unto God, a workman that needeth not to be ashamed, rightly dividing the word of truth. But shun profane *and* vain babblings: for they will increase unto more ungodliness (2 Timothy 2:15).

Relax, Be Patient, Be Still, Listen, Await Direction!

The Good Book said these things:

Rest in the Lord, and wait patiently for him . . . (Psalm 36:7).

Be still, and know that I *am* God . . . (Psalm 46:10).

Order my steps in thy word: and let not any iniquity have dominion over me (Psalm 119:133).

My soul *waiteth* for the Lord more than they that watch for the morning: I *say, more than* they that watch for the morning (Psalm 130:6).

My soul, wait thou only upon God: for my expectation is from him. He *is* my rock and my salvation; *he is* my defence; I shall not be moved (Psalm 62:5-6).

Speak, Lord; for thy servant heareth (1 Samuel 3:9).

See also Proverbs 3:5-6; Psalm 19:14; Psalm 139:23; Acts 9:6.

Watch, Continue in Prayer, Give Thanks, Don't Be Anxious!

The Good Book said:

Watch and pray (Matthew 26:41).

Continue in prayer, and watch in the same with thanksgiving (Colossians 4:2).

Giving thanks always for all things unto God and the Father in the name of our Lord Jesus Christ (Ephesians 5:20).

Be not therefore anxious for the morrow; for the morrow will be anxious for itself.
Sufficient unto the day is the evil thereof [Matthew 6:34—part of the Sermon on the Mount (Quoted from the Revised Version)].

See also Philippians 4:6-7.

Write Down the Thoughts That Come!

The Good Book said:

Thus speaketh the Lord God of Israel, saying: Write thee all the words that I have spoken unto thee in a book (Jeremiah 30:2).

And the Lord answered me, and said, Write the vision, and make *it* plain upon tables, that he may run that readeth it (Habakkuk 2:2).

Check the Word to Avoid Self-deception!

The Good Book provides many tests, and this one comes from James 1:17:

Every good gift and every perfect gift is from above, and cometh down from the Father of lights, with whom is no variableness, neither shadow of turning.

Believe!

The Good Book said:

And all things whatsoever ye shall ask in prayer, believing, ye shall receive (Matthew 21:22).

See also: Mark 11:24; 1 John 5:14-15.

Obey!

The Good Book said:

Obey my voice, and I will be your God, and ye shall be my people; and walk ye in all the ways that I have commanded you, that it may be well unto you (Jeremiah 7:23).

But be ye doers of the word, and not hearers only, deceiving your own selves (James 1:22).

It Works!

The Good Book said:

The effectual fervent prayer of a righteous man availeth much
(James 5:16).

I will instruct thee and teach thee in the way which thou shalt
go; I will guide thee with mine eye (Psalm 32:8).

Commit thy way unto the Lord; trust also in him; and he shall
bring *it* to pass (Psalm 37:5).

See also: Proverbs 3:5-6; Romans 8:14; 2 Corinthians 5:7.

Elements of Quiet Time

Ye Must Be Born Again!

Though modern A.A. history has carefully avoided the details, the
prerequisite surrender in Akron and even in New York meant
coming to Jesus Christ as Lord and Savior. There certainly were
many reasons for this: to obtain power, to obtain forgiveness, to
receive God's mercy and grace, to be healed, to gain everlasting
life, *and to be able to hear from God.* Bill Wilson's spiritual
teacher, Sam Shoemaker wrote:

> Now St. Augustine said truly: "We are not born Christians, but
> we become Christians." (*Realizing Religion*, p. 5).

> What you want is simply a vital religious experience. You need
> to find God. You need Jesus Christ (*Realizing Religion*, p. 9).

> God on His part has longed to win us for years. It has been we
> who have been unwilling. We must open ourselves to Him, and
> be prepared to accept all that it will mean to be a child of God
> (*Realizing Religion*, pp. 28-29).

There are many verses to which AAs turned for information on
how to be born again of the spirit of God. See John 3:3-8, 14:6;

Acts 4:7-12, 19:1-6; Romans 10:9; 2 Corinthians 5:17; 1 Peter 1:23.

The following portions of 1 Corinthians 2:9-14 explain exactly why man needs to be born of the spirit of God in order to receive and understand the things of God:

> But as it is written, Eye hath not seen, nor ear heard, neither have entered into the heart of man, the things which God hath prepared for them that love him. But God hath revealed *them* unto us by his Spirit: for the Spirit searcheth all things, yea, the deep things of God. For what man knoweth the things of a man, save the spirit of man which is in him? even so the things of God knoweth no man, but the Spirit of God. Now we have received, not the spirit of the world, but the spirit which is of God; that we might know the things that are freely given to us of God. Which things also we speak, not in the words which man's wisdom teacheth, but which the Holy Ghost teacheth; comparing spiritual things with spiritual. But the natural man [the man of body and soul, but without spirit] receiveth not the things of the Spirit of God: for they are foolishness unto him: neither can he know *them*, because they are spiritually discerned.

Clearing the Receiver

This section will not discuss the Oxford Group's life-changing program. But that program was about life-changing through the power of Jesus Christ. The formula was: Sin is the problem. Jesus Christ is the solution. The result is a miracle.

As long as there were "blocks" to God and other people, the "lens" was unclear. The "receiving set" had to be put in good order by the process of the Five C's: Confidence, Confession, Conviction, Conversion, and Continuance. Then the light could come through.

A Definite, Adequate, Early Time

Time was an important factor in Quiet Time. An hour or more was usual. Setting aside a definite time in the morning, while one was fresh. An adequate time. Adequate to learn about God, to study His will, to petition Him, and to hear from Him. These were the prime differences between today's two minute reflection blurbs and the hour or so early AAs spent with Anne Smith at the Smith home in the wee hours of the morning.

A Quiet, Peaceful, Relaxed Time

Quality time was needed for God. A time of quiet. This could mean in a quiet room, on a quiet porch, or in one's study. An unhurried time. A peaceful setting. One of the guide's Shoemaker recommended said: "Shut the door on the world and all that would distract." (*How to Find Reality in Your Morning Devotions*, p. 3).

Read the Bible

The reason today's "reflections" or "meditations" bear no resemblance to early A.A. is that they discount or ignore the importance of the Bible. The Bible itself said it was a "lamp" and a "light" which enabled understanding. Anne Smith suggested studying the Bible daily. Dr. Bob did study it intensely. Sam Shoemaker said: "Read and know the Bible, and all else, including public worship, will fall into its place" (*Realizing Religion*, p. 62). The Oxford Group said: "Read it through. Pray it in [Ask God to open the Word to you and bring the truth to light]. Write it down [mark your Bible]. Work it out [Be Christlike]. Pass it on [Quickly, go tell]." See *How to Find Reality in Your Morning Devotions*, pp. 1-3; *Foundations for Faith*, 2d ed., pp. 30-31; *Just for Today*, last page.

Use Devotionals Where Needed

The devotionals were ancillary. The Bible was primary. Today, the Bible has been eliminated, and the two minute quip has been substituted for God's Word. Shoemaker wrote:

> *Read before you pray*. Read the Bible systematically. You may find *helpful* the serial books of devotion called Forward Day by Day, or the Upper Room or E. Stanley Jones' "Abundant Living." Use any devotional book that helps you. This draws your mind towards God, and makes you ready to pray [italics added] (*How to Find God*, p. 15).

Praying to God

Praying was stressed. It was called "communion with God." Brother Lawrence passed the last forty years of his life in continuous practice of the presence of God, which he described as a quiet, familiar conversation with Him (*The Practice of the Presence of God*, p. 80); and the Brother Lawrence book was much read as an example of how to pray.

Anne Smith spoke of several categories of prayer: (1) Intercessory prayer: "Pray that Spirit may tell you what to pray for." (2) Petitionary prayer: "Means expression of our wants which we deeply feel. . . . These we submit because He is our Friend. Similarly it would be unnatural not to submit to God the needs of others." (3) Prayers of praise: "adoration and thanksgiving." (4) Prayers for guidance.

To these, one Oxford Group writer added what he called: The Prayer of Attention: "Speak, Lord, for thy servant heareth." Shoemaker reminded of the prayer for "Confession."

Hearing from God

Shoemaker said the distinguishing element of a Quiet Time is listening for the guidance of God. He spoke of praying together, "opening their minds to as much of God as he [the new person] understood, removing first the hindrance of self-will, allowing the Spirit to focus an impression upon the mind, like light upon a camera" (*Children of the Second Birth*, p. 16).

Oxford Group writer Cecil Rose said: "God has a plan. God speaks. But if He is to be heard and His plan is to be known and carried out, man must listen. . . . We are learning to know His voice in our "quiet time." and we recognize it better elsewhere" (*When Man Listens*, pp. 30-34)

Writing Down Thoughts

Oxford Group founder Dr. Frank Buchman often explained the difference between "Guidance" and "Quiet Time." Buchman simply held up a pencil. Quiet Time was about "journalizing" or writing down the thoughts that came to the listener. It was considered an aid to concentration, a reminder of duties to be performed, and a basis for checking thoughts received each morning and through the day.

"Checking" the Guidance

The Oxford Group and early AAs were not so naive as to believe that every thought that came to them in Quiet Time was from God. As they said: Nothing that is unloving, impure, dishonest, or selfish comes from God. Thoughts were to be checked against what the Bible had to say concerning such thoughts, whether they violated the Four Absolutes (honesty, purity, unselfishness and love), and whether they seemed correct to a trustworthy friend who believed in the guidance of the Holy Spirit.

Obeying the "Voice"

Sam Shoemaker wrote the following about John 7:17:

A moral experiment is worth ten times an intellectual investigation in apprehending spiritual truth. Obedience is as much the organ of spiritual understanding as reason. Many people have come into a personal and living faith by trying the experiment which is implied in: "If any man willeth to do his will, he shall know" [from John 7:17, and see *Religion That Works*, p. 86].

Dr. Frank Buchman's obedience saying was legendary:

God alone can change human nature. The secret lies in that great forgotten truth that when man listens, God speaks; when man obeys, God acts (*Remaking the World*, p. 46).

Guidance and the Bible Devotionals

When one speaks about the spiritual roots of A.A., he or she simply must speak about the guidance received via the spirit of God directly from God Almighty. And also about the Bible devotionals that were read daily in the pioneer days.

Revelation from God

As to the guidance of God: Early AAs sought that guidance at every turn. Thus Bill Wilson said this about Dr. Bob in *RHS*, the memorial issue of A.A.'s *Grapevine*:

Dr. Bob always began his day with a prayer and meditation over some familiar Bible verse, then he set about his work in "My Father's vineyard . . . " (p. 30).

Suddenly the ceiling went up. We no longer flew blind. A beacon had been lighted. God had shown alcoholics how it might be passed from hand to hand (p. 8).

Telling the story of how Bill Wilson had written the Twelve Steps, A.A.'s biography *Pass It On* had this to say:

As he started to write, he asked for guidance. And he relaxed.
The words began tumbling out with astonishing speed (p. 198).

So, if one believes that God had a hand in guiding the co-founders
in their spiritual path, as it developed, the founders themselves
certainly confirmed that fact. "Guidance," "Quiet Time," and
asking God for direction were an integral part of early A.A.
thinking and practice.

Daily Reminders from the Devotionals

The devotionals themselves provided daily inspiration concerning
the Bible verses AAs were studying. Here are several that were
often mentioned by the pioneers.

The Upper Room was paramount in importance. It was a
quarterly published by the Methodist Church, and it began its
publication almost the moment A.A. was founded in 1935.
Following is an example from the very first issue, for the day of
April 22, 1935. The topic was guidance. The verse for study was
part of the A.A. legacy:

I will instruct thee and teach thee in the way which thou shalt
go: I will guide thee with mine eye (Psalm 32:8).

The comment begins: "He who created us in His own image
desires that we fulfill His plans for our lives. Are we going His
way, or do we follow our own ways?" The suggested additional
reading is Acts 10. The prayer begins: "Heavenly Father, our
fears vanish when we believe that Thou art near us for friendly
guidance." The thought for the day states: "Ought we not each day
to remember that God constantly seeks through us to guide broken,
troubled lives into spiritual peace and power?"

Throughout the next four years of A.A.'s development, *The
Upper Room* pages laid out the same kinds of ideas on most of the
basic principles AAs were to borrow from the Bible.

The Runner's Bible was very much stressed by Dr. Bob. A
note at its beginning says:

For him who must run and yet would read, and particularly for her who at seventeen has already begun to run, these commands and promises of Holy Writ are gathered and grouped by one who, while running, has felt the need.

In the beginning, the little volume states: "In the Morning will I order my prayer unto Thee." It points out the importance of the Morning Watch, and it quotes many of the verses we have listed above. The topics are these: (1) Statements of Truth: The Godhead; God the Father; The Christ of God; Him that filleth all in all; His image and likeness. (2) The Divine Commands: Walk in love; Rejoice always; In everything give thanks; Fear not, only believe; Get wisdom, Get understanding; Ask and ye shall receive; He that is greatest among you shall be your servant; Forgive and ye shall be forgiven. (3) Promises: Be of Good Cheer, Thy sins be forgiven thee; I will help thee; Behold, I will heal thee; For thine is the power; The Lord shall guide thee continually; Thou shalt walk in thy way safely; All things are yours; Peace be unto you; Happy shalt thou be; The Lord will lighten my darkness.

The importance of these collections of verses in *The Runner's Bible* is that so many of them quote the Book of James (the favorite in early A.A.) and set forth the verses so much a part of the early A.A. philosophy and ideas.

My Utmost for His Highest by Oswald Chambers was popular with Bill Wilson and his wife Lois. It was used by Dr. Bob and his wife Anne. It was popular with Henrietta Seiberling, but it was considered a bit too intellectual by most of the drunks. Nonetheless, Chambers covered for each day many of the verses upon which early AAs drew for ideas. An example is September 26th, titled "The Unblameable Attitude." The page quotes part of Matthew 5:23 in the Sermon on the Mount—which was the inspirational verse for A.A.'s Step Nine. It discusses being reconciled to one's brother. Another example is the Twelfth Step verse popular with many of the pioneers: "If any man be in Christ, he is a new creature: old things are passed away" (an adaptation on October 23 from 2 Corinthians 5:17). June 30 begins "Do it now." It quotes the Eighth Step idea: "Agree with thine adversary quickly." This too is from the Sermon on the Mount—Matthew 5:25.

Other devotionals in common use were Harry Emerson Fosdick's *The Meaning of Prayer*, E. Stanley Jones's *Victorious Living* (mentioned by name in the First Edition of *Alcoholics Anonymous*), and Mary W. Tileston's *Daily Strength for Daily Needs*.

4

The Oxford Group and
Alcoholics Anonymous

It took a long time for Bill Wilson to overcome his wariness of
mentioning A.A.'s very clear roots in the Oxford Group and for
him to give that Group its due. After Oxford Group founder Dr.
Frank N. D. Buchman died in 1961, Bill finally said:

> Now that Frank Buchman is gone and I realize more than ever
> what we owe to him, I wish I had sought him out in recent
> years to tell him of our appreciation (*Pass It On*, p. 387).

In 1941, Bill had requested that Jack Alexander avoid mentioning
"the Oxford Group situation" in his proposed *Saturday Evening
Post* article. Yet Bill conceded: "After all we owe our lives to the
group" (*Pass It On*, pp. 26-27). Just before Buchman died, Bill
made a further acknowledgement, but still credited his friend Sam
Shoemaker. Bill wrote that AAs had learned about moral
inventory, amends for harm down, turning wills and lives over to
God, meditation and prayer, "and all the rest of it" from the
Oxford Group (*The Language of the Heart*, p. 198).

Core Oxford Group Ideas

There have been a number of inadequate, limited descriptions of the core ideas that A.A. borrowed from the Oxford Group. But the picture is not complete unless one realizes that the whole "spiritual program" of A.A.—which is founded on the necessity for a "spiritual experience" or "spiritual awakening"—comes almost completely from the Oxford Group's life-changing program. Fairly stated, the following are the ideas:

About God

God is the Creator, Maker, Father, and Almighty. God has a plan. Man's chief end is to conform to that plan. And man starts with the necessity for believing that God *is*. The very expression in A.A.'s Big Book that "God either is or He isn't" came almost verbatim from the writings of Oxford Group leader The Reverend Sam Shoemaker. Sam Shoemaker and early A.A. were both emphatic in their written suggestions that *suffering people needed to find God now*.

About Sin

The Oxford Group had a simple description for sin. It was whatever blocked a person from God and from other people. Sin was also defined as selfishness, self-centeredness, ego-centricity, the big "I." All terms well known to AAs. Sin, said the Oxford Group, had to be eliminated in order for man to have a relationship with God. The formula for eliminating sin could be described in two different ways. The first was from Frank Buchman: Sin, Jesus Christ, and the result, A Miracle. The second was from Buchman's ideas of Surrender, Soul Surgery (to cut away and eliminate the sin), and the result—a changed or transformed life.

Eliminating Sin through Self-Surrender

The "turning point" in A.A., in Sam Shoemaker's writings, and in the Oxford Group's life-changing program, was often expressed by Sam Shoemaker in a quote from Professor William James, the much admired Harvard psychologist from whom Bill Wilson borrowed some A.A. ideas. Shoemaker said:

> Self-surrender has always been and always must be regarded as the vital turning point of the religious life, so far as the religious life is spiritual and no affair of outer works and ritual and sacraments. One may say that the whole development of Christianity in inwardness has consisted in little more than the greater and greater emphasis attached to this crisis of self-surrender (*Realizing Religion*, p. 30).

The Power through Jesus Christ

People cannot change themselves, said the Oxford Group. The transforming power of Jesus Christ that is gained through being born again of the spirit is absolutely essential. Men and women surrender. They do this by believing in God, seeking God first, and becoming born again of the spirit of God. At the beginning, there was often the simple prayer: "Thy will be done"—from the Lord's prayer in the Sermon on the Mount.

The Life-Changing Five C's

Mankind has a role in establishing the relationship with God. As Shoemaker put it, people suffer from spiritual misery because there is estrangement from God by people who were meant to be His companions. You need a vital religious experience; you need to find God; you need Jesus Christ (said Sam Shoemaker in *Realizing Religion*, p. 9). The "art" of changing lives, said Frank Buchman, could be described in terms of Five C's—Confidence, Confession, Conviction, Conversion, and Continuance (*Life Changers*, p. 169). These five ideas were mentioned in early A.A. and formed the heart of its middle Steps. Confidence meant gaining the confidence of a newcomer through witnessing and then utilizing that Confidence to win a Confession of sins or shortcomings. Conviction was the process of acknowledging that the shortcomings were sins against the ways of God and needed to be eliminated. Conversion involved the submission and humbling in throwing one's self on the mercy of God, and receiving His grace in the form of a new birth—"Christ in you." Finally, there was "Conservation" or "Continuance" which involved the daily contact with God, the experiencing of His deliverance, the witnessing to that deliverance, and the practice of God's own spiritual principles.

Restitution, or Amends

Perhaps especially unique in its emphasis was the idea of making restitution, which the Oxford Group fostered. It listed several Bible segments in support of the idea. But the foundations were in the Sermon on the Mount, which involved agreeing with one's adversary quickly and clearing up the wreckage of the past. This was God's will, said the Oxford Group, and carrying it out was essential to a new relationship with God and with others. The Big Book used virtually the same words on the last page of its basic text (p. 164).

Daily Surrender

Some forget the emphasis the Oxford Group placed on daily watchfulness. This idea was one that Bill Wilson added to the original six steps when he wrote Step Ten. There was to be a daily watchfulness for sin, a daily confession to others, a daily conviction and turning to God for help, a daily making of amends, and a daily concern for others. Love and tolerance were A.A.'s code, and they were Oxford Group and Bible ideas.

Quiet Time

Little needs to be repeated here about the elements of Quiet Time. But daily contact with God was a major part of the Oxford Group life and spiritual growth just as the Eleventh Step is in A.A.'s practice of the principles. This meant Bible study, use of helpful books, prayer, listening, writing down thoughts, checking them, and obeying them. The persistence of these ideas can be found as Dr. Bob firmly stated them in his last major address to AAs in 1948 (*The Co-Founders of Alcoholics Anonymous*, pp. 11-14, 16-18).

Spiritual Awakening, Witness, Practice of Principles

The A.A. terms "spiritual awakening" and "spiritual experience" came straight from the frequent use of those terms by Oxford Group Founder Frank Buchman, by Rev. Sam Shoemaker, and by Oxford Group writers. The terms had to do with "God-consciousness"—a term also mentioned with frequency in the Oxford Group and early A.A.

"Passing it on" was biblical; and Frank Buchman and other Oxford Group people referred to this very thought—pass it on. Jesus Christ emphasized the idea of witness (Mark 16:10-10). Frank Buchman actually used the term "pass it on" (*Remaking the World*, p. x). Shoemaker frequently said: "You have to give it away to keep it"—a term well known in A.A.

Practicing spiritual principles certainly centered around the Oxford Group's Four Absolutes—honesty, purity, unselfishness and love. These Four Absolutes or Four Standards are still mentioned in the Oxford Group today, and also in various parts of A.A. Also incorporated in the principles to be practiced were the "love" principles in 1 Corinthians 13.

Specific Oxford Group Ideas in the Twelve Steps

Step One

"O, God, manage me, because I cannot manage myself." This simple prayer was often mentioned by Frank Buchman, Sam Shoemaker, and Anne Smith. Its counter-part can be found in A.A.'s "Our lives had become unmanageable."

Step Two

Sam Shoemaker wrote of the need for "a Force outside himself, greater than himself" and "a vast Power outside themselves." He insisted that there be a willingness to believe, and that there be a belief in God. The willingness, he said, was wrapped up in the experiment of faith by which a person stepped out on the belief by obeying God and realizing, as Jesus taught in John 7:17, that the believing produced results.

Step Three

The Oxford Group laid the foundation for the A.A. idea that surrender starts with a *decision*. Using language in *Twice-Born Ministers* that was borrowed almost verbatim in A.A.'s Step Three, Shoemaker spoke of "the decision to cast my will and my life on God" (p.34). Then Shoemaker forecast and virtually framed the famous A.A. expression "God as we understood Him." He frequently spoke of "surrendering as much of yourself as you understand to as much of God as you understand" (*Children of the Second Birth*, pp. 27, 47). Using language similar to that in the original Third Step draft, Shoemaker said: "She surrendered to God . . . and . . . turned over to Him her life for His direction" (*Children of the Second Birth*, p. 82).

Step Four

The language of Step Four is Oxford Group. In *Soul Surgery*, Oxford Group writer H. A. Walter pointed to Frank Buchman's insistence that each person "make the moral test" (pp. 43-44). Oxford Group mentor Henry Drummond wrote that man needs to "devote his soul to self-examination, to self-examination of the most solemn and searching kind" (*The Ideal Life*, p. 316). Frank Buchman said: "Moral recovery starts when everyone admits his own faults instead of spot-lighting the other fellow's" (*Remaking the World*, p. 46).

Step Five

Oxford Group writer Stephen Foot explained as to confession: "The first step for me was to be honest with God, the next to be honest with men" (*Life Began Yesterday*, p. 11). Howard Walter wrote: "Be ready to confess your own shortcomings honestly and humbly" (*Soul Surgery*, p. 57).

Step Six

In *The Venture of Belief*, Oxford Group activist Philip Marshall Brown wrote: "To summarize the various stages of spiritual adventure; first, the will to believe; second, the honest facing and sharing of all conscious sin; third, the complete surrender of self to God; and, fourth, the willingness to obey His will" (p. 36).

Step Seven

In *I Was a Pagan*, Bill Wilson's friend and Oxford Group co-worker Victor Kitchen wrote: "It takes the power of God to remove the desire for these indulgences" (p. 143). Kitchen also said: "I then and there admitted my inability to quit of my own will and asked God to take charge of the matter" (p. 74). He also said: "God . . . satisfied unsound desire by removing the desire itself" (p. 73).

Step Eight

"God cannot take over my life unless I am willing," said Cecil Rose in *When Man Listens* (p. 17). Oxford Group writer Jack Winslow said: "A further point in the moral challenge which the Oxford Group presents is that known as restitution, viz. putting right, as far as in our power, wrongs committed in the past" (*Why I Believe in the Oxford Group*, p. 31).

Step Nine

Cecil Rose said: "These first steps of restitution are absolutely necessary if I am to start the new life clear with God and other people. . . . [The] great task that is waiting: cooperate with God and to ask God to make us fit for Him to use" (*When Man Listens*, p. 20).

Step Ten

Shoemaker said: "There is need for rededication day by day, hour by hour, by which progressively, in every Quiet Time, the contaminations of sin and self-will are further sloughed off, for they do have a way of collecting" (*The Conversion of the Church*, p. 79). And using language which A.A. seems to have adopted verbatim, Frank Buchman said: "What is the disease? Isn't it fear, dishonesty, resentment, selfishness?" (*Remaking the World*, p. 38).

Step Eleven

Cecil Brown wrote: "They tell of the strength of heart and mind, of the depth of knowledge of life, of the charity and love that are poured into human beings whenever they establish contact with God" (*The Venture of Belief*, p. 24). Stephen Foot said: (1)

"Contact with God is the necessary fundamental condition, and that is made through prayer and listening. . . ." (2) "I will ask God to show me His purpose for my life and claim from Him the power to carry that purpose out" (*Life Began Yesterday*, pp. 13, 11). Victor Kitchen wrote: "I 'emerged' into God-consciousness" (*I Was a Pagan*, p. 43).

Step Twelve

Walter wrote in *Soul Surgery*: "The basis of conversion is the awakening of a new self, and the vital element in this new birth is the dawning of a new affection which dominates the heart" (p. 82). Sam Shoemaker said: "This experience, which I consider was my conversion, brought to me a new kind of life which was entirely new to me" (*Twice-Born Ministers*, p. 55). Long ago, Frank Buchman wrote: "The best way to keep an experience of Christ is to pass it on" (*Remaking the World*, p. x). As to practicing the principles taught in the Sermon on the Mount and elsewhere in the Bible, A. J. Russell wrote: "Moreover, it meant a relentless crusade to induce other men and women not only to believe in the possibility of living the victorious life, but to live it" (*For Sinners Only*, p. 62). Streeter wrote in *The God Who Speaks*: "Christ does not merely teach men what to do, he gives them power to do it" (p. 151).

The Many Oxford Group Expressions AAs Adopted

My title, *The Oxford Group & Alcoholics Anonymous*, contains nearly two hundred Oxford Group expressions which found their way into early A.A. These expressions show how the writings in the Oxford Group not only impacted upon A.A., but in many cases were adopted almost verbatim. Two interesting examples can be found in the A.A. references to the importance of a "group" and to their Society as a "fellowship." Speaking about the Oxford Group, Shoemaker wrote in 1932: "I unhesitatingly say that the

Group is the Church on the march, and that every church should be a Group. The original Church was often called "the Fellowship" (*The Conversion of the Church*, pp. 7-8. The very close parallel between Oxford Group words, phrases, ideas, and principles is, then, probably the major reason why both Bill and Dr. Bob frequently mentioned their early membership in the Oxford Group, also known as "A First Century Christian Fellowship," of which A.A. was an integral part.

5

Sam Shoemaker, "Co-founder" of A.A.

Bill Wilson said these things about the role of Sam Shoemaker in A.A.:

> Every river has a wellspring at its source. AA is like that too. In the beginning, there was a spring which poured out of a clergyman, Dr. Samuel Shoemaker. 'Way back in 1934 he began to teach us the principles and attitudes that afterward came to full flower in A.A.'s Twelve Steps for recovery (*The Language of the Heart*, p. 177).

> The Twelve Steps of A.A. simply represented an attempt to state in more detail, breadth, and depth, what we had been taught—primarily by you. Without this, there could have been nothing—nothing at all. . . . Though I wish the "co-founder" tag had never been hitched to any of us, I have no hesitancy in adding your name to the list! (Letter from Wilson to Shoemaker, dated April 23, 1963).

The Close Personal Association

Had Bill been dealing in specifics, he could have said much more. It is fair to say that Sam Shoemaker commented or taught on just about every item from the Bible, the devotionals, and the Oxford Group that we have covered in the other parts. Sam wrote over thirty books, many sermons, as well as articles and pamphlets whose ideas contributed to A.A.'s Big Book, Twelve Steps, and Fellowship. Sam had a circle of clergy and Oxford Group friends whose books and teachings fed into Wilson's thinking and writing. And Sam himself was closeted in his office with Wilson throughout A.A.'s formative years. Shoemaker mentions Wilson by name in several entries in his (Sam's) personal journals, and he carried on a continuing correspondence with Bill until his (Sam's) death. Over the years, Shoemaker contributed several articles to A.A.'s *Grapevine*, and Wilson asked him to address A.A.'s international conventions in St. Louis and in Long Beach in 1955 and 1960, which Shoemaker did.

Some Major Shoemaker Ideas That Impacted A.A.

There are many words and phrases which Bill Wilson used in A.A. literature that could have come directly from Shoemaker. If they didn't come directly, they can be found in the writings and talks by the Oxford Group people who were close associates of Shoemaker, and in many cases of Wilson himself. These Oxford Group leaders included Dr. Frank Buchman, The Rev. and Mrs. W. Irving Harris, Rowland Hazard, F. Shepard Cornell, Ebby Thacher, The Rev. Howard Blake, Professor Philip Marshall Brown, The Rev. John Potter Cuyler, Jr., The Rev. Sherry Day, Stephen Foot, Eleanor Napier Forde, Loudon Hamilton, Roger Hicks, Victor Kitchen, Garth Lean, The Rev. Ray Purdy, Amelia Reynolds, The Rev. Howard Rose, Kenaston Twitchell, and many others. All of these associates were participants in the "teams," meetings, houseparties, and activities of the Oxford Group with which Bill Wilson was associated from November of 1934 through August of 1937.

The Spiritual Malady: Spiritual Misery

It did not take Bill and Dr. Bob long to realize that the alcoholic suffered from more than a drinking problem. They each concluded he had a spiritual disease; and they believed that when the spiritual malady was cured, the person's drinking problem would be resolved. It would have been miraculously "removed." It would vanish. And, wherever they obtained these ideas—including the notion that "self" was the heart of the spiritual problem—their path had been charted by Sam Shoemaker. He had written:

> Now the thing which is striking about much of the misery one sees is that it is *spiritual misery*. . . . It is the sadness of maladjustment to the eternal things, and this throws out the whole focus of life. Rest cures and exercise and motor drives will not help. The only thing that will help is religion. For the root of the malady is estrangement from God—estrangement from Him in people that were made to be His companions (*Realizing Religion*, pp. 4-5).

> For most men the world is centered in self, which is misery (*Realizing Religion*, p. 11).

> Self-will seems the blackest sin of all, rebellion against God the only hell (*Realizing Religion*, p. 31).

> God is God, and self is not God—that is the heart of it. It is an actual fact that we become God to ourselves unless we have God to believe in: the final reference becomes ourselves (*National Awakening*, p. 48).

The Solution: A Spiritual Experience and Relationship with God

Neither the term "spiritual experience," nor the term "spiritual awakening" can be attributed to Shoemaker alone. For both were common expressions in the Oxford Group—along with the expression "religious experience." But Shoemaker defined the solution in terms AAs will quickly recognize:

> What you want is simply a vital religious experience. You need to find God. You need Jesus Christ (*Realizing Religion*, p. 9).

The conspiracy of silence, about sin, about deliverance, about spiritual experience, has lasted long enough. This generation is frank about other things, and they want the truth about what God does for us (*Twice-Born Ministers*, p. 61).

Do you think a moral and spiritual awakening might be the answer to our needs? . . . President Angell of Yale believes that the fullness of life cannot be achieved "through economic channels solely, but can come only from an awakening ethical and religious spirit." And the President of the United States declares that he doubts "if there is any problem—social, political or economic—that would not melt away before the fire of such a spiritual awakening" (*National Awakening*, pp. 2-3).

We believe entirely that conversion is the experience which initiates the new life. But we are not fools enough to think that the beginning is the end! All subsequent life is a development of a relationship with God which conversion opened (*Children of the Second Birth*, p. 16).

How to Find God

Shoemaker wrote eloquently and often on how to find God. He used terms familiar to AAs.

God is, or He isn't (*Confident Faith*, p. 187).

Let go! Abandon yourself to Him. Say to Him, "Not my will but Thine be done" (*Religion That Works*, p. 19).

Surrender to whatever you know about Him, or believe must be the truth about Him (*The Gospel According to You*, p. 128). [When you are helping and working with another to surrender, this means there will be] opening their minds to as much of God as he understood, removing first the hindrance of self-will, allowing the Spirit to focus an impression upon the mind, like light upon a camera exposed (*Children of the Second Birth*, p. 47). Convince the person to "surrender as much of himself as he could, to as much of Christ as he understood" (*Children of the Second Birth*, p. 25).

Give in, admit that I am God, high over nations, high over the world (*National Awakening*, p. 45; Psalm 46:10—Moffatt's translation)

Except a man be born again, he cannot see the kingdom of God. . . . Ye must be born again. . . . A man is born again when the control of his life, its center and its direction pass from himself to God (*National Awakening*, pp. 56-57; John 3:3-8).

This was probably the origin of the Big Book ideas that God is or He isn't, and that one simply surrenders to as much of God as he understands and essentially says: "Thy will be done." When he obeys God's will, he becomes conscious that God exists and knows from his experience what God has done for him.

The Experiment of Faith

For atheists and agnostics, much of the A.A. basic text involves an experiment of faith: An experiment that moves the beginner out of unbelief into believing and finally into knowing God and the will of God. The experiment commenced with "willingness." These ideas can be found presented by the Oxford Group's life-changing program. Shoemaker was not their only proponent, but he certainly wrote much about the experiment and founded his ideas on John 7:17. He said:

Prayer is the heart of the discovery of the will of God. . . . But that kind of prayer is impossible without radical and basic surrender to the will of God first. "If any man willeth to do his will"—this means, no grudging concession to God, but whole-hearted allegiance and the co-operation of one's whole self—"he shall know."

The Twelve Steps were designed to move the pioneers toward "God-consciousness." Shoemaker set out some specific ideas for starting the journey. He said that finding real security meant a faith in God which includes an experiment:

> It lies in believing that God is, that he has a plan, and that He will reveal that plan to us. It lies in fitting in with that plan ourselves, and finding that God will take care of us when we dare to make that experiment (*National Awakening*, p. 40).

There were, said Shoemaker, three basic elements in making the experiment:

> The first is a belief in God (*National Awakening*, p. 41; Hebrews 11:6).

> The second thing is utter preoccupation with God's plan. "Seek ye first the Kingdom of God, and His righteousness" (*National Awakening*, p. 41; Matthew 6:33).

> The third thing is that God can tell you your part in that plan (*National Awakening*, p. 42).

How to Know the Will of God

Once one has surrendered himself to as much of God as he understands, and has sincerely tried to obey as much of God's will as he knows, God will reveal more. The promise was in the Sermon on the Mount, said Shoemaker:

> Not everyone that saith unto me, Lord, Lord, shall enter into the kingdom of heaven; but he that doeth the will of my Father who is in heaven (*Religion That Works*, p. 65; Matthew 7:31).

He pointed out that there is a general will of God, and there is a particular will of God (*A Young Man's View of the Ministry*, p. 78). He elaborated:

We find God's general will in the Scriptures (*The Conversion of the Church*, p. 49).

We want something much more direct. We want to know that God can and does speak directly to the human heart. The reason why some of us believe in guidance, at least in theory, is that the Old and New Testaments are full of instances of it, as specific as you please (*The Conversion of the Church*, p. 50)

. . . [T]he one thing in religion that matters most: a real hold on God, and a real knowledge of His will by genuine revelation (*The Conversion of the Church*, p. 63).

Surrender to God's will, which is the heart of faith, is summed up in the question, "Lord, what wilt thou have me to do? . . . We have got to wipe the slate clean, and then ask Him to write His will upon it" (*A Young Man's View of the Ministry*, p 80). God give us the grace to ask: "Lord, what wilt thou have me to do?" (*Religion That Works*, p. 65; Acts 9:6).

Religion today is largely the imitation of an example, when it ought to be the hearing of a Voice (*The Conversion of the Church*, p. 62).

What Eli said to Samuel that day is the last word in spiritual advice: ". . . thou shalt say, Speak Lord; for thy servant heareth." There is active faith, and the listening attitude, and the patience which waits for the emergence of God's plan, all wrapped up in one" (*National Awakening*, p. 83; 1 Samuel 3:9).

You Have to Give It Away to Keep It

Shoemaker had lots to say about witnessing. But he possibly authored, and certainly spoke many times about the importance of sharing your experience of God with others. Some Oxford Group people have called Sam the best life-changer of all. His expression of "giving it away" has become a part of A.A. lingo. He said:

The only way to keep religion is to give it away. Give what you can right away; it will increase as you give it (*One Boy's Influence*, p. 15).

The best way to keep what you have is to give it away, and no substitute has ever been found for personal Christian witness (*They're on The Way*, p. 159).

We must begin giving away what we have, or we shall lose it (*How to Become a Christian*, p. 80).

Get them into the stream of God's will and God's grace, till they ask Him to use them to help reconcile others. They will not keep this unless they give it away (*The Church Alive*, p. 139).

From Spiritual Malady to Spiritual Experience

It should be apparent from the Oxford Group discussion that the Twelve Steps were virtually in place before Bill Wilson wrote them. They covered each Step idea from the unmanageable life and the need to find God to the conclusion that there had been an experience of God which needed to be passed on and utilized in the practice of daily affairs. Some of Shoemaker's titles such as *The Gospel According to You* almost put those ideas in the same order in which A.A. presents them. And they must have been in such order when Bill began his journey. You can see them spelled out in Bill's story as he described the events in his drinking, then his meeting with Ebby Thacher, and then his surrender at Towns Hospital (which was followed by his "hot flash" experience), and then another visit by Ebby. You can also find the sequence of ideas in the much more detailed manuscripts by Bill, which the author discovered and has set forth in *Turning Point: A History of Early A.A.'s Spiritual Roots and Successes*.

6

Anne Smith: "Mother of A.A.," Founder, Dr. Bob's Wife

Anne's Role

Unfortunately, A.A.'s official histories have all but ignored Anne Ripley Smith's vital role in the movement. So have other histories. Sometimes Anne was virtually relegated, along with Henrietta Seiberling, to the position of "one of the ladies who poured coffee." And this vacuum has left A.A. without any detailed picture, told by one of A.A.'s own, of what the real spiritual elements and program were as A.A. was being developed. We will touch briefly on what others said about Anne and then turn primarily to the spiritual journal which she assembled and shared from A.A.'s spiritual beginnings in Akron in 1933 until the Big Book was published in 1939.

Bill Wilson said . . .

> She was, quite literally, the mother of our first group, Akron Number One. Her wise and beautiful counsel to all, her insistence that the spiritual come before anything else, her unwavering support of Dr. Bob in all his works; all these were virtues which watered the uncertain seed that was to become A.A. . . . In the full sense of the word, she was one of the

57

founders of Alcoholics Anonymous (*The Language of the Heart*, pp. 353-54).

Then [after the first few weeks] came a lull on the Twelfth Step front. In this time Anne and Henrietta [Seiberling] infused much needed spirituality into Bob and me (*The Language of the Heart*, pp. 356-57).

Reading . . . from her chair in the corner, she would softly conclude [her reading of the Bible with], "Faith without works is dead." As Dr. Bob described it, they were "convinced that the answer to our problem was in the Good Book. To some of us older ones, the parts that we found absolutely essential were the Sermon on the Mount, the 13th chapter of First Corinthians, and the Book of James." The Book of James was considered so important, in fact, that some early members even suggested "The James Club" as a name for the Fellowship (*Pass It On*, p. 147).

Others said . . .

[Lois Wilson, Bill's wife said] Annie's part in the formation of AA and consequently in the foundation of Al-Anon should never be forgotten, especially by Family Group members" (*Lois Remembers*, p. 96).

[Arch T., founder of A.A. in Detroit said] I had been taken off the streets and nursed back to life by Anne Smith. I was not only penniless and jobless, but too ill to get out of the house during the day and hunt for work. So great was Anne's love and so endless her patience with me, so understanding her handling of me, that ten months later, I left a new man. . . . (*DR. BOB and the Good Oldtimers*, p. 115).

[Bob E., a pioneer, said] She had a quiet, soft way of making you feel at home. I shared a good many of my life's problems with her. She read the Bible and counseled me (*DR. BOB*, pp. 116-17).

[Dan K. said] Anne always looked to the newcomers (*DR. BOB*, p. 223).

[Betty S., Anne's daughter-in-law] I doubt that any minister in any given week could have counseled more people, prayed with more people. In times of trouble, people rushed to her (*DR. BOB*, p. 304).

[Florence B. of Akron said] Anne was "evangelist, nurse, salesman, employment bureau, all in one. . . ." Anne's personal religion was simple and workable. She never sought to rewrite the Bible nor to explain it. She just accepted it (*The Akron Genesis of Alcoholics Anonymous*, pp. 108-09).

Anne Smith's Spiritual Journal, 1933-1939

From the earliest years of A.A.'s beginnings in Akron, Anne Smith assembled, compiled, and shared with AAs and their families at the Smith home the contents of her spiritual journal. Of this, Akron oldtimer John R. said:

> Before one of these meetings [in Dr. Bob's home], Anne used to pull out a little book [her spiritual journal] and quote from it. We would discuss it. Then we would see what Anne would suggest from it for our discussion (*The Akron Genesis*, p. 110).

Anne's journal has lain, virtually unstudied, in the A.A. Archives in New York and at Bill Wilson's home at Stepping Stones. But it is priceless in the information it supplies, the ideas it propounds, and the history it records. It was kept by Anne in her own hand and partly typed up for her by her daughter Sue Smith Windows. It covers Anne's notes about the Bible, the Oxford Group, the literature AAs read, and almost every Step idea that was later adopted and placed in the Big Book in 1939.

Almost all of what we cover here comes directly from the contents of Anne's journal, but one cannot see the full picture without studying our report of it in *Anne Smith's Journal, 1933-1939*.

Twelve Step Ideas

If Bill and Bob were developing the Twelve Step ideas, Anne was certainly learning them, teaching them, recording them, or all three. While we will not cover material already set forth in the sections about the Bible, the Oxford Group, and Shoemaker, we need to sketch out the Step ideas as Anne expressed them.

Step One. Anne twice specifically mentioned the "manage me" prayer that was popular with Buchman and Shoemaker ("O Lord manage me, for I cannot manage myself").

Step Two. Using language resembling that in A.A.'s Second Step, Anne said: "A stronger power than his was needed. God provided the power through Christ, so that we could find a new relationship with God."

Step Three. "Try to bring a person to a decision to 'surrender as much of himself as he knows to as much of God as he knows.' Stay with him until he makes a decision and says it out loud." She added, "Surrender is a complete handing over of our wills to God, a reckless abandon of ourselves, all that we have, all that we think, that we are, everything we hold dear, to God to do what he likes with. . . ."

Step Four. "It is absolutely necessary to face people with the moral test. . . . Criticism born of my own projection. Something wrong in me. Unless I can crystalize the criticism, I had better look for the mote in my eye. . . . Make the moral test. 4 Standards [the Four Absolutes]. . . . Why I had been absolutely honest but not living [it]. . . . Resentments to be faced and set right. . . . Fear and worry are atheism. . . . Just a glimpse of self-centered life."

Step Five. "Confess your faults one to another. . . . I must share to be honest with God, myself & others."

Step Six. "Be willing to ask God where I am failing and to admit sin."

Step Seven. [speaking of sins such as selfishness, dishonesty, and pride] "Christ can only remove them and replace with a new quality of life. Read Romans 12. . . . Do not pretend you can go on lifting yourself by your own boot straps. In all humility to God, "What would thou have me to do?". . . . I'm wrong Father. . . show me the way."

Steps Eight and Nine. "Any restitution I won't make. . . . Resentments to be faced and set right. . . . Restitution to be made. . . . Help them make a list of things. . . . God can make me willing in the day of His power."

Step Ten. "Check your life constantly by the four absolutes." "Our lives will be one continuous surrender: surrender to God of every difficulty that confronts us, each temptation, each spiritual struggle, laying before Him either to take away or to show us in their proper spiritual proportions." "Be willing to ask God where I am failing and to admit sin."

Step Eleven. (1) *Prayer*: "Intercessory prayer—pray that Spirit may tell you what to pray for. . . . A way to find God's will not to change it." "Petitionary prayers. . . . These we submit not because we distrust His goodness or desire to bend His Will but because He is our Friend. . . . Correct me—direct—praise—adoration and thanksgiving. Romans II." (2) *Guidance*: "Guidance is the principle of the Bible, its very structure." "We must be in such relationship with God that He can guide us. . . . Specifically, guidance comes through intelligent knowledge of the Bible, through conscience, through circumstance. . . . guidance is thinking plus God." "I will lead you and guide you in all truth, and bring all thoughts to your remembrance (John)." (3) *Listening*: "Watch your thoughts. Your thoughts can come from three sources. 1. Subconscious. 2. The devil. 3. God." (4) *Bible study and reading*: "Let all your reading be guided. . . . Of course the Bible ought to be the main Source Book of all." (5) *Quiet Time*: "Effective Quiet Time: 1. Objective, God and obedience. 2. Attentive prayer and being willing to act immediately. 3. Stillness and surrender of all known sins." In addition, there are many many specific comments about prayer, listening, reading, and so on that should be read to get the full flavor and depth of Anne's teaching.

Step Twelve. (1) *Having had a spiritual experience*: "A general experience of God is the first essential, the beginning. We can't give away what we haven't got. We must have a genuine contact with God in our present experience." (2) *Carrying the message*: "Giving Christianity away is the best way to keep it." "When we have that [a general experience of God], witnessing to it is natural, just as we want to share a beautiful sunset." (3) *Practicing the principles*: "Start the person on a new life with simple, concrete and definite suggestions, regarding Bible study, prayer, overcoming temptation and service to others." "God's answer to materialism is a basis of Christian living that lifts above material things." "Claim from God humility, patience, courage, faith and love."

Anne's Recommended Reading

Anne was very specific in the type of books she recommended. The Bible came first. All reading should be "guided," she said. Then she recommended books on the life of Christ, books on life-changing, books on prayer, books by Sam Shoemaker and E. Stanley Jones and Toyohiko Kagawa, and other books that would enrich the spiritual lives of those she counseled. We will be discussing these books in a later part.

The Oxford Group Ideas

It would be repetitious to go over the Oxford Group ideas we covered in the Oxford Group part. Suffice it to say that every single Oxford Group idea was covered in Anne's journal. She demonstrated a thorough familiarity with the concepts and taught them to others.

The Bible

Salted throughout Anne's Journal are verses and comments about the Bible. She not only recommended it and studied it and read it to others. She related it to the ideas in the Oxford Group and in the Step ideas we have covered.

Why "Mother" and "Founder?"

Anne Smith was not just an interested bystander to Bill and Bob's meetings and work with drunks. It was Anne who got Bob interested in the Oxford Group. Bob's interest sparked his three year quest in the Bible. Anne attended Oxford Group meetings with Dr. Bob and Bill. She had been a teacher, and she *taught*. She taught Bill and Bob from the Bible, the Oxford Group literature, and the Christian literature of that day. She housed and fed and counseled and assisted the drunks that, at times, overwhelmed the modest home in Akron. She wrote the materials down in her journal and taught others from that. She communicated with many on the phone. She worked with the alcoholics and with their families. People came to the Smith home early in the morning for what they called "spiritual pablum." It involved Quiet Time with Anne; and there was Bible study, prayer, meditation, reading, and discussion. Most importantly, Anne placed great store in working with newcomers. A great many of the comments in her spiritual journal deal with how to work effectively with others in winning them to Christ and helping them change their lives.

One who is not familiar with the specifics in Anne's journal cannot truly say he or she has fully absorbed or fully reported the spiritual history or the spiritual beginnings or even the spiritual principles of A.A. For it was Anne, along with Henrietta Seiberling, T. Henry and Clarace Williams, and a handful of Oxford Group people that were able to provide sober, sympathetic, loving, intelligent spiritual menu items for the new program of recovery. Anne's journal covers it all in minute detail! Yet, as her son Robert put it in the Foreword to *Anne Smith's Journal*: "The way that help was given, steadfast love was shown, was so subtle, so unassuming, so void of self seeking that only a few know of the debt that is owed."

7

The Books and Materials
Early AAs Read

Early AAs were readers. The Bible was the written word of God. The daily devotionals were written guides. Oxford Group people wrote. Sam Shoemaker wrote. Anne Smith wrote. And there were a great many books available for reading. Dr. Bob was an avid reader, and so was his colleague Henrietta Seiberling. Every pioneer A.A. meeting had tables set out in T. Henry's house where literature was available. Dr. Bob recommended and circulated many books. He kept a journal which recorded the books loaned, and he quizzed the alcoholics on the Bible and on the written materials they had borrowed from him. Whatever their proclivity for reading, early AAs all attested to the presence of the Bible and *The Upper Room*. They mentioned *The Runner's Bible*. They mentioned E. Stanley Jones books. They mentioned Henry Drummond's *The Greatest Thing in the World*. They mentioned *My Utmost for His Highest*. They mentioned James Allen's *As a Man Thinketh*. They mentioned the popular Glenn Clark books, Emmet Fox books, and Harry Emerson Fosdick books. There were religious books, and almost every one elaborated on some aspect of ideas AAs were borrowing from the Bible and the Oxford Group for their basic principles.

There was plenty of material on the Bible, prayer, healing, divine guidance, the Sermon on the Mount, 1 Corinthians 13, and the Book of James. There were Oxford Group/Shoemaker materials on finding God, changing lives, conversion, the guidance of God, fellowship, witness, and the teachings of Jesus. There has, perhaps, never been a fellowship with such diversity of subject matter at the immediate beck and call of its participants. Nor with such encouragement of its study by the "leadership."

Dr. Bob's Library

Dr. Bob and everyone that knew him well in the early A.A. days spoke of the immense amount of reading he did. He read the Bible through three times and studied it daily. As he put it:

> I read everything I could find, and talked to everyone who I thought knew anything about it (*DR. BOB*, p. 56).

> [Of the Oxford Group books and the Bible] . . . I had done an immense amount of reading they had recommended. I had refreshed my memory of the Good Book, and I had had excellent training in that as a youngster (*The Co-Founders of Alcoholics Anonymous*, p. 11-12).

> [To his son, "Smitty"] Well, I should know something, I've read for at least an hour every night of my adult life—drunk or sober (*RHS*, pp. 37-38).

DR. BOB and the Good Oldtimers reported:

> For the next two and a half years [After January, 1933], Bob attended Oxford Group meetings regularly and gave much time and study to its philosophy. . . . He read the Scriptures, studied the lives of the saints, and did what he could to soak up the spiritual and religious philosophies of the ages (p. 56).

Dr. Bob's daughter told the author that her father frequently stayed up late into the night studying the Bible (*Dr. Bob's Library*, p. 13).

With the foregoing comments as a start, the author was privileged to see the huge number of books that Dr. Bob had assembled, read, studied, and circulated. The author saw them in the home of Dr. Bob's daughter, Sue Smith Windows, in Akron; and he saw them in the home of Dr. Bob's son, Robert Smith, in Nocona, Texas. Many of the books had Dr. Bob's name and address in them with the notation "Please return." *Dr. Bob's Library* lists the materials in detail. But it is important to cover here the subject matter to show how much light it was able to shed on the ideas A.A. pioneers were studying and borrowing.

The Bible

This aspect of Dr. Bob's reading was considered so important that his Bible was donated to the King School Group (A.A. Number One), and it is taken to the podium at the beginning of each meeting, to this very day—a ceremony the author personally witnessed in the company of Dr. Bob's daughter Sue.

Books about the Bible

In the family's possession are *God's Great Plan, A Guide to the Bible* and *The Fathers of the Church*. It is also likely that Dr. Bob read an Oxford Group pamphlet by Roger Hicks (who was one of the Oxford Group people in Akron in 1933) titled *How to Read the Bible*. Also *An Outline of the Life of Christ* by Shoemaker's assistant minister The Reverend W. Irving Harris (written in 1935). Also *The Lord's Prayer and Other Talks on Prayer from The Camps Farthest Out* by one of Bob's favorite authors Glenn Clark (written in 1932). Without a doubt, we know that Dr. Bob read Emmet Fox's book *The Sermon on the Mount*.

Christian Classics

The *Confessions of St. Augustine, The Imitation of Christ* by Thomas a Kempis, and *The Practice of the Presence of God* by

Brother Lawrence were all owned by Bob and were frequently quoted by the writers whose books Bob read.

The Life of Jesus Christ

Anne Smith recommended reading at least one book on the life of Christ a year for a while, commenting that even more would be better. Dr. Bob's daughter confirmed that Dr. Bob read these. They included: *Jesus of Nazareth: A Biography* by George A. Barton, *The Life of Jesus Christ* by The Rev. James Stalker, *Studies of the Man Christ Jesus* by Robert E. Speer, *The Jesus of History* by T. R. Glover, *The Manhood of the Master* and *The Man from Nazareth* by Harry Emerson Fosdick, and *Jesus and Our Generation* by Charles Whitney Silkey. Most of these were quoted in the source books Dr. Bob read.

Daily Bible Devotionals

These devotionals have been mentioned before. They include *Daily Strength for Daily Needs* by Tileston, *My Utmost for His Highest* by Chambers, *The Runner's Bible* by Nora S. Holm, *The Upper Room*, *Victorious Living* and *Abundant Living* by E. Stanley Jones, *Handles of Power* by Lewis L. Dunnington, *I Will Lift up Mine Eyes* by Glenn Clark, *The Meaning of Prayer* by Harry Emerson Fosdick. And probably the highly recommended Oxford Group pamphlets: *How to Find Reality in Your Morning Devotions* by Donald W. Carruthers, *The Guidance of God* by Eleanor Napier Forde, and *The Quiet Time* by Howard J. Rose.

Books on Prayer

Dr. Bob was intensely interested in the efficacy of prayer, and his library bespeaks this interest. Among his many books about the subject of prayer were Glenn Clark's *The Soul's Sincere Desire*, Starr Daily's *Recovery*, Mary Baker Eddy's *Science and Health with Key to the Scriptures*, Charles and Cora Filmore's *Teach Us to Pray*, Emmet Fox's *Getting Results by Prayer*, Gerald Heard's *A Preface to Prayer*, Frank Laubach's *Prayer (Mightiest Force in the World)*, Charles M. Layman's *A Primer of Prayer*, William R. Parker's *Prayer Can Change Your Life*, and F. L. Rawson's *The Nature of True Prayer*.

Books on Healing

There is no doubt that Dr. Bob and his wife relied on the healing power of God. That fact is adequately reported in A.A.'s own histories. But the collection of their books, and the remarks in Anne Smith's Journal show that they owned and read the following: *Christian Healing* by Charles Filmore, *Healing in Jesus Name* by Ethel R. Willitts, and *Heal the Sick* by James Moore Hickson.

The Sermon on the Mount

Dr. Bob's interest in Jesus's sermon was exemplified not only by the many times he studied and quoted it, but also by the foregoing books as well as the following specific studies of the Sermon on the Mount: *Studies in the Sermon on the Mount* by Oswald Chambers, *The Christ of the Mount* by E. Stanley Jones, *The Sermon on the Mount* by Emmet Fox, and *The Soul's Sincere Desire* and *I Will Lift Up Mine Eyes* by Glenn Clark.

Love

Anne Smith devoted four pages of her spiritual journal to Toyohiko Kagawa's treatise on love, titled, *Love: The Law of Life*. Dr. Bob often recommended Henry Drummond's *The Greatest Thing in the World*—a study of the famous love chapter in the Bible, 1 Corinthians 13. Anne often quoted 1 John 4:8—"God is love;" and Dr. Bob frequently spoke of God as a God of love. He summarized A.A.'s ideas as being, in their essence, "love and service."

The Oxford Group

Dr. Shoemaker's books of the 1920's and 1930's were, of course, Oxford Group books, but the author found in the possession of Dr. Bob's family the following books written by other Oxford Group people: *For Sinner's Only* by A. J. Russell, *He That Cometh* by Geoffrey Allen, *Soul Surgery* by Howard A. Walter, *What is The Oxford Group?* by the Layman with a Notebook, *Life Changers* by Harold Begbie, *Twice Born Men* by Harold Begbie (written before the Group was formed), *New Lives for Old* by Amelia Reynolds, and *One Thing I Know* by A. J. Russell. Anne Smith recommended some of these as life-changing stories. Also some of the Shoemaker titles written for that purpose. It seems apparent from Dr. Bob's remarks about the immense amount of Oxford Group literature he had read and the immense amount of reading he did that his Oxford Group reading included many more than the foregoing titles.

Samuel M. Shoemaker, Jr.

Moreover, one could not, as Dr. Bob said, claim he had read an immense amount of Oxford Group literature, without having read many Shoemaker books. Shoemaker was the most prolific Oxford Group writer, was in touch with Oxford Group people in Akron, and was a close friend of Bill Wilson's. Therefore, though the following were the Shoemaker books the author found in possession of Dr. Bob's family, there must have been many others: *Children of the Second Birth, Confident Faith, If I Be Lifted Up, The Conversion of the Church, Twice-Born Ministers*, and *One Boy's Influence*. There were also popular Shoemaker pamphlets, titled *Three Levels of Life* and *What If I Had but One Sermon to Preach?*

Quiet Time Books

Dr. Bob and Anne, and even Bill and Lois Wilson practiced Quiet Time. And the Smiths were well versed in a number of books on the subject. Some were previously mentioned. The following were also popular: *When Man Listens* by Cecil Rose, *God Does Guide Us* by W. E. Sangster; *The God Who Speaks* by B. H. Streeter; *How Do I Begin?* by Hallen Viney; and *When I Awake* by Jack C. Winslow.

William James and Carl Jung

Bill, Bob, and many early A.A.'s read Professor William James's *The Varieties of Religious Experience* (cited by name in A.A.'s Big Book) and Dr. Carl Gustav Jung's *Modern Man in Search of a Soul*. Jung was later called a "founder" of A.A. as was William James.

Other Spiritual Source Books

We will cover our bibliographies in a moment. But here there should be a list of some particularly popular spiritual books early AAs read and which were read by Dr. Bob as well: James Allen's *As A Man Thinketh*; Glenn Clark's *Fishers of Men*, *Two or Three Gathered Together*, *How to Find Health Through Prayer*, and *Touchdowns for the Lord*; Harry Emerson Fosdick's *The Meaning of Service*, *The Meaning of Faith*, *As I See Religion*, *On Being a Real Person*, and *A Great Time to be Alive*; Emmet Fox's *Find and Use Your Inner Power*, *Power Through Constructive Thinking*, *Alter Your Life*, *You Must be Born Again*, *The Great Adventure*, and *Your Heart's Desire*; the many E. Stanley Jones books; Charles M. Sheldon's *In His Steps*; *In Tune with the Infinite* by Ralph Waldo Trine; *Psychology of a Christian Personality* by Ernest M. Ligon; and *Religion Says You Can* by Dilworth Lupton.

Bibliographies

It is not fruitful here to list every book that early AAs read, particularly the Oxford Group and Shoemaker books. But the bibliographies in the following books by Dick B. will provide complete data on all the books believed to have been available and read: (1) *Dr. Bob and His Library*; (2) *The Akron Genesis of Alcoholics Anonymous*; (3) *The Oxford Group & Alcoholics Anonymous*; (4) *New Light on Alcoholism: God, Sam Shoemaker, and A.A.*; (5) *Good Morning!: Quiet Time, Morning Watch, Meditation and Early A.A.*; (6) *Turning Point: A History of Early A.A.'s Spiritual Roots and Successes*; and the most complete and up-to-date is (7) *The Books Early AAs Read for Spiritual Growth*, 7th Edition.

What Oldtimers Said

Some books and pamphlets were very frequently mentioned by A.A.'s pioneers. They were: the Bible, *The Upper Room*, *My Utmost for His Highest*, *The Runner's Bible*, the Glenn Clark books, the E. Stanley Jones books, James Allen's *As a Man Thinketh*, Henry Drummond's *The Greatest Thing in the World*, the Emmet Fox books, Harold Begbie's books, two Lewis Browne books, William James, Carl Jung, the Oxford Group literature, and Sam Shoemaker's books.

These are mentioned in A.A. histories. And they were mentioned in pamphlets and bulletins put out by A.A. offices and groups. They were also mentioned by many of the surviving families and pioneers the author interviewed.

What Did the Literature Contribute?

Many of the core ideas that AAs adopted were ideas that were covered in depth by many different books and materials they read.

Materials about Finding God

AAs were told by Sam Shoemaker, by the Oxford Group, and by their own literature that they needed to find God—and find Him now! Sam Shoemaker wrote on this topic a great deal. So did Leslie D. Weatherhead in books that Bill Wilson owned or may have owned. So did the other writers.

Materials Defining a Spiritual Experience and Awakening

Throughout Bill Wilson's leadership in A.A., he talked much of his famous "hot flash" experience. He pointed to William James's book *The Varieties of Religious Experience* as a validation of what had occurred to him. It is fair to say that neither Dr. Bob nor most AAs ever had anything like Bill's experience. But their reading did define for them what it meant to be converted, to have a conversion experience, to experience the presence of God, and so on.

Understanding God

Shoemaker said you could understand and know God by following Jesus Christ's suggestion in John 7:17—by conducting an "experiment of faith." Once AAs abandoned the Bible, the discussions of the Creator, and their reliance on coming to God through His Son, they began to lose understanding of God. They began talking of a higher power which could be a group, a lightbulb, a door knob, a chair, and nonsense which could not be found in early A.A. nor in the literature early AAs read.

Knowing God's Will

If early AAs wanted to know God's instructions on faith, believing, prayer, study of His Word, forgiveness, healing, deliverance, love, restitution, service, resentment, fear, selfishness, dishonesty, their literature was replete with road maps to pertinent sections of the Bible and teachings about these things.

Moral Standards

Early A.A. was not about "relationships anonymous." Whether they read the Bible, the Ten Commandments, or the Four Absolutes, AAs were given much instruction on how to behave in accordance with God's will. This is true today in only a very limited way.

Quiet Time and Meditation

Early AAs were the recipients of specific information on the biblical origins of Quiet Time on what Quiet Time was, and on how to practice it through Bible study, helpful books, prayer, listening, checking, and so on. Lacking that information today, AAs have been subjected to a barrage of "meditation" and "reflection" materials by writers who have put new spins, new time-saving squibs, and a wide variety of private interpretation on what had originally been understood as a substantial period of communion with God.

Life-Changing

To this very day, A.A.'s basic text speaks of the alcoholic's need to *change*. Early AAs were given specifics on what they were to *change from*, where to obtain the *power to change*, and what they were to *change to*.

Techniques for Effective Witness

There was no shortage of specific information in early A.A. as to *what the message was*, *how to carry it*, and *what to do with the newcomer*. If they simply looked to the Book of Acts and the commentaries about it, they were well supplied. Anne Smith so suggested.

The Importance of Fellowship

Though they may not realize it today, AAs received a rich body of instruction concerning the body of Christ, from the Book of Acts and the many Christian materials they read. They learned the intended meaning of the fellowship of the Spirit, and how God worked with His children where two or three were gathered together.

The foregoing are just a few of the topics covered in the hundreds of books, devotionals, pamphlets, and articles available for the taking by early AAs.

8

Utilizing A.A.'s Spiritual Roots Today

The Dilemma

There are a number of challenging questions that present a dilemma for those who wish to know or attempt to define what A.A. stands for today. Such people may include AAs themselves, other Twelve Step fellowships, churches and clergy, and the recovery community. Here are some points that may leave them wondering:

Bill Wilson's Comments

Bill Wilson said:

A.A. should always give full credit to its several well-springs of inspiration and . . . should always consider these people among the founders of our Society (Kurtz, *Not-God*, p. 323, n. 33).

A.A. was not invented! (*As Bill Sees It*, p. 67).

Who invented AA? It was God Almighty that invented A.A. (Sam Shoemaker's record of Bill Wilson's November 9, 1954 address at the Commodore Hotel in New York; Episcopal Church Archives, Texas).

As a society we must never become so vain as to suppose that we have been the authors and inventors of a new religion. We will humbly reflect that each of A.A.'s principles, *every one of them*, has been borrowed from ancient sources. . . . Let us constantly remind ourselves that the experts in religion are the clergymen; that the practice of medicine is for physicians; and the we, the recovered alcoholics, are their assistants (*Alcoholics Anonymous Comes of Age*, pp. 231-32).

We are only operating a spiritual kindergarten in which people are enabled to get over drinking and find the grace to go on living to better effect (*As Bill Sees It*, p. 95).

The problem of the Steps has been to broaden and deepen them, both for newcomers and oldtimers. But the angles are so many, it's hard to shoot them rightly. We have to deal with atheists, agnostics, believers, depressives, paranoids, clergymen, psychiatrists, and all and sundry. How to widen the opening so it seems right and reasonable to enter there and at the same time avoid distractions, distortions, and the certain prejudices of all who may read, seems fairly much of an assignment (*Pass It On*, p. 354).

A.A.'s Retired Archivist Said

Frank M., A.A.'s just-retired archivist at General Services in New York, has frequently said:

Whenever a civilization or society perishes, there is always one condition present. They forgot where they came from [often heard by the author].

Yet even before Dr. Bob died, Bill seemed increasingly pressured by several major issues that had surfaced in the course of A.A.'s shift from Akron to New York in terms of spiritual ideas, thinking, and emphasis.

The Contrasting Factors

As Lois Wilson Saw Them

Bill's wife Lois said of Bill's writing of the Big Book and A.A.'s abandonment of specific mention of A.A.'s biblical and Christian origins:

> Finally it was agreed that the book should present a universal spiritual program, not a specific religious one, since all drunks were not Christian (*Lois Remembers*, p. 113).

> Well, I didn't have much use for the Oxford Group; I didn't think I needed "conversion" (Kurtz, *Not-God*, p. 314, n. 58).

> [The] Oxford Group kind of kicked us out (*Pass It On*, p. 174).

Roman Catholic Concerns

There was another issue—Roman Catholic distaste for the Oxford Group. A.A. Historian Ernest Kurtz has said that Father John C. Ford, S.J. is a significant figure in the history of A.A.; that he was America's leading Roman Catholic moral theologian in the 1950's; and that he was a frequent writer on the moral problems of alcoholism and alcoholics. Father John Ford met Bill Wilson at Yale in 1943, and Wilson became impressed with Ford as a writer. In consequence, Wilson sought Ford's editorial assistance for A.A.'s *Twelve Steps and Twelve Traditions* (published in 1952 after Dr. Bob's death) and A.A.'s *Alcoholics Anonymous Comes of Age* (published in 1957). The following facts deserve mention:

> [John Cuthbert Ford, S.J. said] . . . I recalled the early 1950's, when I taught at the Yale School of Alcohol Studies, edited *Twelve Steps and Twelve Traditions* and *A.A. Comes of Age* for Bill Wilson, and met Sister Ignatia and Dr. Bob Smith (Darrah, *Sister Ignatia*, p. x).

[Father Ford's main concern with the texts was] "too explicit MRA attitudes" (Kurtz, *Not-God*, p. 323, n. 31).

[Father Ford wrote in 1960] Catholic participation in MRA was ably discussed by R. Bastian, S.J. and J. Hardon, S.J., about two years ago. . . . The authors unhesitatingly reject active cooperation of Catholics in this movement. MRA is a religious movement with fundamentally Protestant, theological orientation, and involves Catholics in serious dangers to their faith (N.C.C.A. "Blue Book", Vol 10, 1960: "Moral Re-Armament And Alcoholics Anonymous").

[Writing to Sam Shoemaker on June 14, 1957 about John Ford's A.A. editing work, Bill Wilson said] He [Father Ford] went over *Twelve Steps and Twelve Traditions* with a fine-tooth comb and is most solicitous that we never get into a jam with the [Roman Catholic] church. He is one of our very best under-cover agents (Episcopal Church Archives, Austin, Texas).

[In one of several lengthy letters to Father Ford, Bill wrote Ford on May 14, 1957] Please have my deepest appreciation for the careful pre-publication survey you have made of our book, "A.A. Comes of Age", from the theological point of view. No one could agree more fully than I on the principle that we should avoid every possibility of theological dispute which might result in a justification for declaring Alcoholics Anonymous a heresy. What you have done might well make much difference in later time. Needless to say I have transferred nearly all your suggestions to the new book, hedging on a few points only (Episcopal Church Archives, Austin, Texas).

Atheist Hoopla

One can seriously question just how many atheists, Jews, Hindus, and Moslems were participants in A.A.'s earliest years. But Bill Wilson later gave "atheists" a great audience. Question: Were the people he mentioned even atheists? One person was Bill's partner Hank Parkhurst who was actually an Oxford Group point man in

New Jersey—a fact verified when the author examined the Shoemaker-Parkhurst correspondence in the Episcopal Church Archives in Texas. The other "atheist" was James Burwell. Granted, Burwell originally "flabbergasted" Bill "by denouncing God at our meetings." But Bill was later to point out to a distinguished Yale audience that Burwell had read the Bible one day at a point of despair, had then seen Bill and another involved in prayer and meditation, and had thereafter managed to get sober for the first time in five years of trying. Nonetheless, Bill wrote in *A.A. Comes of Age*:

> At first they [Parkhurst and Burwell] wanted the word "God" deleted from the book entirely. Henry had come to believe in some sort of "universal power," but Jimmy still flabbergasted us by denouncing God at our meetings. . . . What Henry, Jimmy, and company wanted was a *psychological* book which would lure the alcoholic in. Once in, the prospect could take God or leave Him alone as he wished (*A.A. Comes of Age*, p. 163).

A.A. legend has it that Jimmy Burwell invented the phrase "God as we understood Him" and that this phrase was inserted to placate the atheists and open A.A.'s doors. The first part of the claim was never, to the author's knowledge, authenticated by Bill himself. The fact is that surrendering to God "as you understand Him" was a well-known and long-used Oxford Group phrase and that Bill retained the word "God" in one form or another more than four hundred times even in later editions of the Big Book. When Bill wrote his chapter to agnostics, he pointed out, "And it means, of course, that we are going to talk about God" (First Edition, *Alcoholics Anonymous*, p. 57).

Treatment and Therapy Jabber

As the years moved on, and therapy and treatment moved in, a new lingo crept into the Twelve Step scene: "abuse," "acceptance," "addiction," "chemical dependency," "child

within," "codependency," "committees," "cross-talk," "denial,"
"dry drunk," "enabler," "fake it till you make it," "feelings,"
"Good Orderly Direction," "group therapy," "guilt," "HALT,"
"higher power," "higher power is the A.A. group," "higher power
is a tree," "higher power is a light bulb," "inner child," "in
recovery," "intervention," "ism," "Keep It Simple Stupid,"
"relapse," "renewal," "self-help," "shame," "spiritual, not
religious," "spirituality," "stinking thinking," "substance abuse,"
"support group," "tapes," "therapeutic community," "therapy,"
"victim," and many many more. Some were descriptive. Some
were helpful. Some were nonsense. Some were called
"psychobabble." See some contrasting examples in: (1) *The
Recovery Book*; (2) Robertson, *Getting Better Inside Alcoholics
Anonymous*; (3) Hazelden, *A Spiritual Odyssey*; (4) Clinebell,
Basic Types of Pastoral Care Counseling, (5) *Daily Reflections*;
and (6) Ragge, *More Revealed: A Critical Analysis of Alcoholics
Anonymous and the Twelve Steps*.

Publishing Additions

Finally, out of A.A.'s own publishing organization, came a flood
of ideas that bear no resemblance to any of the early spiritual
principles we have discussed above. For examples, see *Turning
Point: A History of Early A.A.'s Spiritual Roots and Successes*, pp.
5-8, 161-62: a "higher power" that can be "Him, Her, or It," a
"lightbulb," a "chair," a "tree," a Group Of Drunks, "Good," or
nothing at all.

Conservative Christian Recoil

As "any god" became more and more synonymous with "higher
power" in A.A., some Christian writers: 1) Rejected A.A.
(Playfair, *The Useful Lie*), 2) Condemned A.A. (Bobgans, *Twelve
Steps to Destruction* and Burns, *Alcoholics Anonymous Unmasked*),
3) Proposed some "Christian" alternatives—sometimes called
"Christ-centered Twelve Step Groups" (Bartosch, *Overcomers*

Outreach: A Bridge to Recovery, Chambers, *Two Tracks-One Goal*, and Doyle, *In Step with God*).

Where Lies the Answer?

Does A.A. bury its Christian roots because not all AAs are Christians? Does A.A. ignore the fact that its basic ideas came from the Bible because not everyone respects the Bible? Does A.A. gloss over its hundreds of borrowed ideas, phrases, and practices from the Oxford Group and Sam Shoemaker because some Roman Catholic clergy didn't like the Oxford Group? Does A.A. turn God into an dumb idol, a group, or an "it" because someone thinks that will attract newcomers? Does A.A. surrender its biblical/Christian history to manufactured words and ideas that come from outside A.A.

Or, does A.A. endeavor to understand itself better, to learn why it was so successful in the beginning, and take pains to avoid being so "inclusive" that it excludes no self-made religion, no half-baked prayers, and no absurd names for God? Does A.A. ignore the clergy, the church, and the religious community of its roots by surrendering to ideas propounded by Bill Wilson's wife, some dissenting religious writers, two or three outspoken atheists, the fears of treatment programs, and just plain market appeal? These are not wholly accurate descriptions of the pressure factors, but one needs to bear in mind that A.A. developed something between 1935 and 1939 that worked! Depending upon which documentation one prefers, AAs who really tried in that early period attained a seventy-five percent success record (*Alcoholics Anonymous*, 3rd ed, p. xx), an eighty percent success record (Kurtz and Ketcham, *The Spirituality of Imperfection*, pp. 109-10), a ninety-three percent success record (*DR. BOB and the Good Oldtimers*, p. 261), or a one-hundred percent success rate among non-psychotics (*The Jack Alexander Article about AA*, p. 15).

As soon as his thinking began to clear enough to wonder how A.A. started, the author began to prefer the success rate of yesteryear. In the earliest published draft of their proposed basic text (the multi-lith volume), AAs proclaimed "Rarely have we seen a person fail who has thoroughly followed our path" (p. 26). That was the phrase that caught the author's attention. Though most of the personal stories in that volume have since been removed, those original stories talked of a path which involved a "Heavenly Father" and expressed pity for atheists, agnostics, skeptics, or prideful people who refused to accept the formula in the book. See the Personal Stories, p. 6: God (pp. 11, 15-16, 18-20, 26, 41-42, 48, 55, 68, 73, 79); Christ (p. 15), Divine help (p. 19), Our Father in heaven (p. 29), Father (p. 75) the Bible (p. 19, 79).

The success rate of yesteryear was explained again and again in A.A.'s *DR. BOB and the Good Oldtimers.* These were the golden years. They involved God, the Bible, prayer, Quiet Time, surrenders to God (actually acceptance of Jesus Christ as Savior), Christian literature, Christian fellowship, and daily Bible devotionals.

There is an answer as to whether A.A. should bury its Biblical and Christian history or relearn and study it. A.A. has had no problem hashing and rehashing the supposed relevance of Washingtonian mistakes, though the events occurred a century and a half ago. Yet A.A. virtually ignores it more recent, direct, and relevant roots involving events barely more than half a century old. The real answer concerning A.A. history lies in how much value one places on the Biblical principles and the success rate these principles produced when factors are compared to the hodge-podge of fellowship prattle that abounds today.

In their recent title discussing A.A.'s program of recovery versus fellowship ideas today, Joe and Charlie point to the early success rate, to today's diminished success rate, and to their belief that drunks haven't changed, alcohol hasn't changed, the Big Book hasn't changed, but the fellowship *has.* These active, recovered A.A. veterans say:

> The only thing that has really changed is the fellowship itself. We believe that this is a big problem in many AA meetings today. It's a serious problem, too, because far fewer people are

recovering from their illness (*A Program for You: A Guide to the Big Book's Design for Living*, p. 15).

And How Can You Use the History of Early A.A.'s Roots Today?

Combine Big Book Study with Historical Roots Study!

Few recovered AAs today lack respect for A.A.'s basic text, *Alcoholics Anonymous*. That text contains a description, albeit edited and changed over the years, of how the early AAs *recovered*. It describes "the steps they took." It suggests these steps as a program of recovery. And it very definitely contains specific instructions on "how to take" most of these steps; and where the instructions are not specific, details are nonetheless there for those who care to look for them. In fact, a study of the Big Book will demonstrate that the entire program of recovery is explicitly described in the first chapter, *Bill's Story*.

The author learned early on that he was getting little helpful information on either the Big Book or the Steps from Big Book meetings, Step Study meetings, or the other types of meetings he was attending daily. His sponsor and grand-sponsor, though dedicated AAs, did not seem to have the capacity to instruct and perhaps did not even have an understanding of how the Big Book instructed its readers in taking the Steps.

Finally, he attended his first Joe and Charlie Big Book Seminar in Sacramento, California. From this detailed, line-by-line, humorous, and analytical study, he learned a great deal about A.A.'s Big Book. He does not agree today with all the teaching, but he does believe that *all* of it was extremely useful. It focused the student on the Big Book and what Joe and Charlie believed to be its plan. The Seminar was so useful, in fact, that the author attended it several more times and succeeded in getting most of his sponsees to attend. Today, that material is available in written and in taped form. But the most significant thing for the author was that the seminar always began with a discussion of A.A.'s beginnings and how the Big Book was written.

Though the Big Book Seminar history presentation was informative, it was far too scanty for those in search of the spiritual roots—a fact that has several times resulted in the author's being invited to Sacramento to make his books available during the seminar period. And the absence of specific details is one reason why the author undertook his research, travel, interviews, and writing.

The first suggestion here, therefore, is that every AA—every AA who wants to understand recovery *and* tap into A.A.'s vital ideas about God, the Bible, forgiveness, healing, deliverance, prayer, meditation, and Christian standards that inspired the pioneers—should learn A.A.'s true spiritual roots when he or she is learning the Big Book.

Without such study, it is too easy to slip into all the pitfalls and pressures that were previously outlined.

Put the Good Book First on the Study List

A.A. has been so busy tar and feathering the Oxford Group for the last fifty years that it has derailed attention from *A.A.'s primary source, the Bible.*

Most critics of A.A.'s spiritual roots focus on the shortcomings of Oxford Group Founder Frank Buchman or upon Roman Catholic criticism of Moral Re-Armament or upon the fact that AAs left the Oxford Group in the very late 1930's. They ignore the fact that *A.A. was founded on the Bible*, not the Oxford Group. Oxford Group ideas *came* from the Bible. A.A. ideas *also* came from the Bible. But these similarities are far from making the two origins identical.

AAs *should know* by now that A.A.'s basic ideas were taken from the Bible. Dr. Bob said so explicitly (*The Co-Founders of Alcoholics Anonymous: Biographical Sketches, Their Last Major Talks*, pp. 13-14). These ideas, which were derived from the Bible, came from Bible study, use of daily Bible devotionals, Quiet

Time observances that involved Bible study, Christian literature of all kinds—including the Roman Catholic writings of St. Augustine, Thomas a Kempis, Brother Lawrence—and Anne Smith's Journal. All these contained comments about and references to the Bible. Furthermore, if Sam Shoemaker was regarded by Bill Wilson as the teacher of A.A.'s Oxford Group concepts, one should remember that Sam's *major focus* was on the Bible, not the Oxford Group per se. The Oxford Group, for Sam, was a vehicle for bringing people to Christ, not the source of the idea. Sam was an Episcopal Clergyman, and he left the Oxford Group in 1941 primarily because he did not want to give up his own primary focus upon his church and the liturgy and methods of that church.

The second major suggestion for understanding A.A. by using its roots, therefore, is that one can understand A.A. best by pulling out the Bible. Then by doing a line-by-line study of important parts of the Bible (particularly Matthew 5 to 7, 1 Corinthians 13, and the Book of James). The student should focus on those words, phrases, and ideas which the author has specifically identified as biblical in origin and rooted in the specific portions of the Bible covered here.

Study first. Accept help. Understand afterward. That's the approach to Big Book study that worked for the author. That is the approach to the Bible that God suggested (John 5:39; Acts 17:11, 8:26-35; 2 Timothy 2:15). It is an approach to understanding A.A.'s spiritual program of recovery that can lift the fog.

Learn the Early Technique for Quiet Time

In their haste for a quick fix and easy reading, some AAs have allowed writers to burden them down with meditation after meditation after meditation book. And each book seems to get shorter and farther away from the Bible.

Learn *why* Anne Smith said the Bible is the main source book. It is the book that explains who God is. It is the book which tells what God's will is. It is the book that points out how to come to God, or—if you prefer—to "find" God. It is the book which contains God's promises, God's admonitions, and God's suggestions for communications to and from Him. "Thy will be done" means very little if one does not know where and how to find God's will. Yet Jesus Christ taught that doing "the will of my Father which is in heaven" was key to entry into the kingdom of heaven (Matthew 7:21). Jesus said in a prayer to God that he had spoken God's Word (the words of God he had received by revelation) and that it (collectively, the word) was truth (John 17:14, 17). Then Jesus declared unequivocally that "the truth shall *make you free*" (John 8:32, italics added).

Once one understands the technique for Quiet Time—Bible study; helpful books; prayers for help and guidance; prayers of thanksgiving and praise; prayers for healing and forgiveness; and listening for God's messages—he or she can begin to reap the rewards of communion with God. Jesus admonished against vain repetitions that simply displayed ego to a Father who already knew the needs and how to take care of them. Anne Smith explained that to early AAs.

Examine Anne Smith's Spiritual Journal

It is not difficult to get far afield of A.A.'s original spiritual program of recovery if one ignores the precise material Anne Smith wrote, shared, and taught to the pioneers and their families. The interrelationship of the Bible, the Oxford Group life-change, the Christian literature, and daily Bible devotionals becomes clear from reading Anne's comments.

Look on the Oxford Group for Understanding, Not Theology

A.A.'s debt to the Oxford Group lies in a number of areas. The Oxford Group brought special focus on the need for God, the guidance of God, the importance of fellowship, the importance of witnessing, and the necessity for practicing Christian principles as a way of life. A.A. bought these ideas whole hog, whatever they called them. Hence one can look to the writings of Sam Shoemaker and of the Oxford Group people for specific explanations of specific ideas A.A.'s adopted. The ideas are still there. God is there. The need for God is there. The need to quit playing God is there. Guidance is there. The Four Absolutes (perhaps minus purity) are there. Restitution is there. Continuance is there. Confession is there. Bill thought Conversion was there. Confidence is there. And Conviction had better be there. Fellowship is there. And witnessing is there. One does not need to agree with or fear the Oxford Group theology to know their ideas are important if one hopes to understand how A.A.'s "spiritual awakening" can possibly be the result of taking the steps. There is no message to carry if one has not learned and understood it. There are no principles to practice if one does not know what they are or what they are for.

Get an Understanding of God As He Understands Himself

In the Bible, God describes Himself in a way that we can understand. He is the Creator. He is the Maker. He is Spirit, not a man. He is light, not darkness. He is love, not hate. He is Father, if we choose to be born of His spirit. He is Almighty, if we want power. He heals, if we are sick. He forgives, if we sin. He delivers, if we are in trouble. He guides, if we do not know the way or want to be told. He promises health, prosperity, abundance, an everlasting life, and a way out of alcoholism, if we care to seek and entrust our lives to Him for care and direction. He is the God of peace, comfort, consolation, grace, mercy, and love, if that is what we want. That is how He understands and explains Himself. And the modern-day absurdities can't hold at candle to that.

If AAs are told to find God *now*, and they certainly are—in emphatic terms by their own basic text, then why settle for anything less than the "God of our fathers," of which Wilson and Smith spoke, and the "God of A.A.'s own founders" upon which Wilson and Smith relied?

"WHO ARE YOU TO SAY THERE IS NO GOD?" Those words, in capital letters, can be found on page 69 of the First Edition of *Alcoholics Anonymous*. What ever happened to that idea? "What seemed at first a flimsy reed, has proved to be the loving and powerful hand of God," said page 38. Whatever happened to that idea? "The central fact of our lives today is the absolute certainty that our Creator has entered into our hearts and lives in a way which is indeed miraculous," said page 36. Whatever happened to that idea? "But my friend (Ebby Thacher) sat before me, and he made the point-blank declaration that God had done for him what he could not do for himself," said pages 20-21. Whatever happened to that idea? "As to two of you men, whose stories I have heard, there is no doubt in my mind that you were 100% hopeless, apart from Divine help," said page 55. Whatever happened to that idea? "We never apologize to anyone for depending upon our Creator?," said page 81. Whatever happened to that idea?

Virtually nothing has happened to any of these ideas. They are not lost, but they seem to be slipping away. Most of the phrases are still present in A.A.'s basic text today. They are part of the program of recovery. It's just that people are scared to death to talk about them in many of today's meetings and discussions—to talk about God, the Creator, Divine help, the hand of God, and the way in which pioneers placed total reliance upon these.

The way to use the roots today is to "Go tell." Sam Shoemaker taught:

> Men run from your arguments about God, they will not listen to your elaborate explanations; but when you tell them what life was without God, and then tell them what it is with Him, their hearts, as John Wesley said, are "strangely warmed," and their minds also are strangely persuaded (*National Awakening*, p. 28).

Then, as he usually did, Shoemaker pointed to the Bible and to this reply Jesus gave to the disciples of John when they asked if Jesus was the person who was to come:

Jesus answered and said unto them, Go and shew John again those things which ye do hear and see: The blind receive their sight, and the lame walk, the lepers are cleansed, and the deaf hear, the dead are raised up, and the poor have the gospel preached to them (Matthew 11:4-5).

At another point, Shoemaker repeated an idea well-known in the Oxford Group *and* in early A.A.: "The Gospel was originally 'news,' not 'views'" (*The Conversion of the Church*, p. 73).

Nobody ever recovered from alcoholism by relying upon a tree. Nobody ever recovered from alcoholism by praying to a group. Nobody ever recovered from alcoholism by meditating upon a lightbulb. Alcoholics may be sick. But they are not stupid. Tell the AAs of today the facts. Tell them the early success statistics. Offer them the opportunity to learn more. And let *them* decide where they wish to place their reliance for recovery and deliverance from the deadly disease from which they suffer.

The End

About the Author

Dick B. writes books on the spiritual roots of Alcoholics Anonymous. They show how the basic and highly successful biblical ideas used by early AAs can be valuable tools for success in today's A.A. His research can also help the religious and recovery communities work more effectively with alcoholics, addicts, and others involved in Twelve Step programs.

The author is an active, recovered member of A.A.; a retired attorney; and a Bible student. He has sponsored more than seventy men in their recovery from alcoholism. Consistent with A.A.'s traditions of anonymity, he uses the pseudonym "Dick B."

He has had fourteen titles published: *Dr. Bob and His Library*; *Anne Smith's Journal, 1933-1939*; *The Oxford Group & Alcoholics Anonymous: A Design for Living That Works*; *The Akron Genesis of Alcoholics Anonymous*; *The Books Early AAs Read for Spiritual Growth*; *New Light on Alcoholism: God, Sam Shoemaker, and A.A.*; *Courage to Change* (with Bill Pittman); *The Good Book and The Big Book: A.A.'s Roots in the Bible*; *That Amazing Grace: The Role of Clarence and Grace S. in Alcoholics Anonymous*; *Good Morning!: Quiet Time, Morning Watch, Meditation, and Early A.A.*; *Turning Point: A History of Early A.A.'s Spiritual Roots and Successes, Hope!: The Story of Geraldine D., Alina Lodge & Recovery*, *Utilizing Early A.A.'s Spiritual Roots for Recovery Today*, and *By the Power of God: A Guide to Early A.A. Groups & Forming Similar Groups Today*. The books have been the subject of newspaper articles, and have been reviewed in *Library Journal, Bookstore Journal, For a Change, The Living Church, Faith at Work, Sober Times, Episcopal Life, Recovery News, Ohioana Quarterly, The PHOENIX, MRA Newsletter*, and the *Saint Louis University Theology Digest*.

Dick is the father of two married sons (Ken and Don) and a grandfather. As a young man, he did a stint as a newspaper reporter. He attended the University of California, Berkeley, where he received his A.A. degree, majored in economics, and was elected to Phi Beta Kappa in his Junior year. In the United States Army, he was an Information-Education Specialist. He received his A.B. and J.D. degrees from Stanford University, and was Case Editor of the Stanford Law Review. Dick became interested in Bible study in his childhood Sunday School and was much inspired by his mother's almost daily study of Scripture. He joined, and was president of, a Community Church affiliated with the United Church of Christ. By 1972, he was studying the origins of the Bible and began traveling abroad in pursuit of that subject. In 1979, he became much involved in a Biblical research, teaching, and fellowship ministry. In his community life, he was president of a merchants' council, Chamber of Commerce, church retirement center, and homeowners' association. He served on a public district board and was active in a service club.

In 1986, he was felled by alcoholism, gave up his law practice, and began recovery as a member of the Fellowship of Alcoholics Anonymous. In 1990, his interest in A.A.'s Biblical/Christian roots was sparked by his attendance at A.A.'s International Convention in Seattle. He has traveled widely; researched at archives, and at public and seminary libraries; interviewed scholars, historians, clergy, A.A. "old-timers" and survivors; and participated in programs on A.A.'s roots.

The author is the owner of Good Book Publishing Company and has several works in progress. Much of his research and writing is done in collaboration with his older son, Ken, who holds B.A., B.Th., and M.A. degrees. Ken has been a lecturer in New Testament Greek at a Bible college and a lecturer in Fundamentals of Oral Communication at San Francisco State University. Ken is a computer specialist.

Dick is a member of the American Historical Association, Maui Writers Guild, and The Authors' Guild. He is available for conferences, panels, seminars, and interviews.

Dick B.'s Historical Titles on Early A.A.'s Spiritual Roots and Successes

Dr. Bob and His Library: A Major A.A. Spiritual Source (Third Edition)
Foreword by Ernest Kurtz, Ph.D., Author, *Not-God: A History of Alcoholics Anonymous*.
A study of the immense spiritual reading of the Bible, Christian literature, and Oxford Group books done and recommended by A.A. co-founder, Dr. Robert H. Smith. Paradise Research Publications, Inc.; 156 pp.; 6 x 9; perfect bound; $15.95; 1998; ISBN 1-885803-25-7.

Anne Smith's Journal, 1933-1939: A.A.'s Principles of Success (Third Edition)
Foreword by Robert R. Smith, son of Dr. Bob & Anne Smith; co-author, *Children of the Healer*.
Dr. Bob's wife, Anne, kept a journal in the 1930's from which she shared with early AAs and their families ideas from the Bible and the Oxford Group. Her ideas substantially influenced A.A.'s program. Paradise Research Publications, Inc.; 180 pp.; 6 x 9; perfect bound; 1998; $16.95; ISBN 1-885803-24-9.

The Oxford Group & Alcoholics Anonymous (Second Edition)
Foreword by Rev. T. Willard Hunter; author, columnist, Oxford Group activist.
A comprehensive history of the origins, principles, practices, and contributions to A.A. of "A First Century Christian Fellowship" (also known as the Oxford Group) of which A.A. was an integral part in the developmental period between 1931 and 1939. Paradise Research Publications, Inc.; 432 pp.; 6 x 9; perfect bound; 1998; $17.95; ISBN 1-885803-19-2. (Previous title: *Design for Living*).

The Akron Genesis of Alcoholics Anonymous (Newton Edition)
Foreword by former U.S. Congressman John F. Seiberling of Akron, Ohio.
The story of A.A.'s birth at Dr. Bob's Home in Akron on June 10, 1935. Tells what early AAs did in their meetings, homes, and hospital visits; what they read; how their ideas developed from the Bible, Oxford Group, and Christian literature. Depicts roles of A.A. founders and their wives; Henrietta Seiberling; and T. Henry Williams. Paradise Research Pub.; 400 pp., 6 x 9; perfect bound; 1998; $17.95; ISBN 1-885803-17-6.

The Books Early AAs Read for Spiritual Growth (Fwd. by John Seiberling; 7th Ed.)
The most exhaustive bibliography (with brief summaries) of all the books known to have been read and recommended for spiritual growth by early AAs in Akron and on the East Coast. Paradise Research Publications, Inc.; 126 pp.; 6 x 9; perfect bound; 1998; $15.95; ISBN 1-885803-26-5.

New Light on Alcoholism: God, Sam Shoemaker, and A.A. (2d Ed.)
Forewords by Nickie Shoemaker Haggart, daughter of Rev. Sam Shoemaker; and Mrs. W. Irving Harris.
A comprehensive history and analysis of the all-but-forgotten specific contributions to A.A. spiritual principles and practices by New York's famous Episcopal preacher, the Rev. Dr. Samuel M. Shoemaker, Jr.—dubbed by Bill W. a "co-founder" of A.A. and credited by Bill as the well-spring of A.A.'s spiritual recovery ideas. Paradise Research Publications, Inc.; 672 pp.; 6 x 9; perfect bound; 1999; $24.95; ISBN 1-885803-27-3.

The Good Book and The Big Book: A.A.'s Roots in the Bible (Bridge Builders Ed.)
Foreword by Robert R. Smith, son of Dr. Bob & Anne Smith; co-author, *Children of the Healer*.
The author shows conclusively that A.A.'s program of recovery came primarily from the Bible. This is a history of A.A.'s biblical roots as they can be seen in A.A.'s Big Book, Twelve Steps, and Fellowship. Paradise Research Publications, Inc.; 264 pp.; 6 x 9; perfect bound; 1997; $17.95; ISBN 1-885803-16-8.

That Amazing Grace: The Role of Clarence and Grace S. in Alcoholics Anonymous
Foreword by Harold E. Hughes, former U.S. Senator from, and Governor of, Iowa.
Precise details of early A.A.'s spiritual practices—from the recollections of Grace S., widow of A.A. pioneer, Clarence S. Paradise Research Pub; 160 pp.; 6 x 9; perfect bound; 1996; $16.95; ISBN 1-885803-06-0.

Good Morning!: Quiet Time, Morning Watch, Meditation, and Early A.A. (2d Ed.)
A practical guide to Quiet Time—considered a "must" in early A.A. Discusses biblical roots, history, helpful books, and how to. Paradise Research Pub; 154 pp.; 6 x 9; perfect bound; 1998; $16.95; ISBN: 1-885803-09-5.

Turning Point: A History of Early A.A.'s Spiritual Roots and Successes
Foreword by Paul Wood, Ph.D., President, National Council on Alcoholism and Drug Dependence.
Turning Point is a comprehensive history of early A.A.'s spiritual roots and successes. It is the culmination of six years of research, traveling, and interviews. Dick B.'s latest title shows specifically what the Twelve Step pioneers borrowed from: (1) The Bible; (2) The Rev. Sam Shoemaker's teachings; (3) The Oxford Group; (4) Anne Smith's Journal; and (5) meditation periodicals and books, such as *The Upper Room*. Paradise Research Publications, Inc.; 776 pp.; 6 x 9; perfect bound; 1997; $29.95; ISBN: 1-885803-07-9.

Inquiries, orders, and requests for
catalogs and discount schedules
should be addressed to:

Dick B.
c/o Good Book Publishing Company
P.O. Box 837
Kihei, Maui, Hawaii 96753-0837
1-808-874-4876 (phone & fax)
email: dickb@dickb.com

Internet Web Site: "http://www.dickb.com"

Other Dick B. Historical Titles on Early A.A.

Order Form

Qty.

Send: ___ *By the Power of God: A Guide to Early A.A.*   @ $16.95 ea. $___
          Groups & Forming Similar Groups Today

          Paradise Research Publications, Inc.; 258 pp.; 6 x 9; perfect
          bound; 2000; ISBN: 1-885803-30-3.

   ___ *Utilizing Early A.A.'s Spiritual Roots for Recovery*   @ $14.95 ea. $___
          Today

          Paradise Research Publications, Inc.; 106 pp.; 6 x 9; perfect
          bound; 1999; ISBN: 1-885803-28-1.

   ___ *The Golden Text of A.A.: God, the Pioneers, and*   @ $14.95 ea. $___
          Real Spirituality

          Paradise Research Publications, Inc.; 94 pp.; 6 x 9; perfect
          bound; 1999; ISBN: 1-885803-29-X.

                                          Subtotal $___

Shipping and Handling (within the U.S.)   Shipping and Handling $___
     Add 10% of retail price (minimum $3.75)
                                       Total Enclosed $___

Name: _____ (as it appears on your credit card, if using one)

Address: _____   E-mail: _____

City: _____   State: ___   Zip: _____

CC Acct. #: _____   **Circle:** MC VISA AMEX Exp. ___

Tel.: _____   Signature _____

Please mail this Order Form, along with your check or money order, to: Dick B., c/o Good Book Publishing Company, P.O. Box 837, Kihei, HI 96753-0837. Please make your check or money order payable to "**Dick B.**" in U.S. dollars drawn on a U.S. bank. Please contact us for Shipping and Handling charges for orders being shipped outside of the United States. If you have any questions, please phone or fax: 1-808-874-4876. Dick B.'s email address is: dickb@dickb.com. The "**Dick B. [Internet] Web Site on Early A.A.**": "http://www.dickb.com".

How to Order Dick B.'s Historical Titles on Early A.A.

Order Form

Qty.

Send:

___ *Turning Point* (a comprehensive history)	@ $29.95 ea.	$_____
___ *New Light on Alcoholism* (Sam Shoemaker)	@ $24.95 ea.	$_____
___ *The Oxford Group & Alcoholics Anonymous*	@ $17.95 ea.	$_____
___ *The Good Book and The Big Book* (Bible roots)	@ $17.95 ea.	$_____
___ *The Akron Genesis of Alcoholics Anonymous*	@ $17.95 ea.	$_____
___ *That Amazing Grace* (Clarence and Grace S.)	@ $16.95 ea.	$_____
___ *Good Morning!* (Quiet Time, etc.)	@ $16.95 ea.	$_____
___ *Anne Smith's Journal, 1933-1939*	@ $16.95 ea.	$_____
___ *Books Early AAs Read for Spiritual Growth*	@ $15.95 ea.	$_____
___ *Dr. Bob and His Library*	@ $15.95 ea.	$_____

	Subtotal $_____

***Shipping and Handling (S & H) ***

Add 10% of retail price (minimum US$3.75). ** U.S. only.
For "The Set," add US$18.67. ** U.S. only   **S & H** $_____
Please call, fax, or email for shipments outside the U.S.

Total Enclosed $_____

Name: _____ (as it appears on your credit card)

Address: _____

City: _____ State: ___ Zip: _____

Credit Card #: _____ (MC VISA AMEX) **Exp.** _____

Tel. #: _____ Signature _____

Email address: _____

Special Value for You!

If purchased separately, the author's ten titles sell for US$191.50, plus Shipping and Handling. Using this Order Form, you may purchase sets of all ten titles for **only US$149.95 per set, plus US$19.15** Shipping and Handling. Please contact us for Shipping and Handling charges for orders being shipped outside of the United States.

Send Order Form (or copy), with check or money order, to: Dick B., P.O. Box 837, Kihei, HI 96753-0837. Please make check or money order payable to "**Dick B.**" in U.S. dollars drawn on a U.S. bank. For questions, please phone or fax: 1-808-874-4876. Our email: dickb@dickb.com. **Dick B.'s Web Site:** "http://www.dickb.com".